# Table of Contents

## Unit 1—Phonemic Awareness

## Unit 2—Phonics and Word Recognition

## Unit 3—Vocabulary and Concept Development

## Unit 4—Reading Comprehension

# As Easy as 1–2–3

**①** **Prepare** the assessment task activity.

**②** **Administer** the task and record the student's performance.

**③** **Reteach** or provide additional practice using the reproducible activity sheet.

## Everything You Need

Each assessment task includes:

- **Scripted instructions**
  for administering the assessment task

- **Full-color mats and cards**
  to engage the student in a specific task

- **Class checklist**
  to record each student's performance

- **Reproducible activity sheets**
  for additional skill practice

## When to Conduct an Assessment

You may choose to use assessment tasks in any of the following ways:

- Assess students at the beginning of the school year to determine individual student skill levels.

- Administer an assessment after a specific skill has been taught to help confirm mastery or need for further instruction.

- Assess students throughout the year to monitor progress. Use the correlation chart on page 6 to correlate assessments with your lesson plans.

**You may also wish to visit www.teaching-standards.com to view how the skills are correlated to your state's standards.**

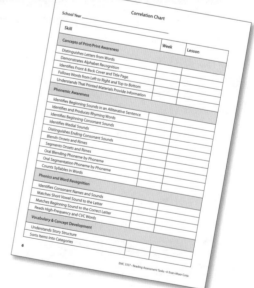

# Preparing an Assessment Task Activity

Assemble each assessment task activity and place it in an envelope.
Store the envelopes in a file box or crate for easy access.

## Materials:

- 9" x 12" (23 x 30.5 cm) large manila envelopes
- scissors
- clear tape
- scripted instructions, manipulatives, class checklist, and activity sheet for the specific assessment task

## Steps to Follow:

1. Remove and laminate the *scripted instruction page*. Tape it to the front of the envelope.

2. Remove and laminate the *manipulatives* (sorting mats, task cards, etc.). Store cards in a smaller envelope or plastic bag.

3. Reproduce the *class checklist*. Tape it to the back of the envelope.

4. Make multiple copies of the *activity sheet* and store them in the envelope.

> Make one copy of the *Individual Student Assessment Checklist* (page 5) for each student in your class. You may wish to keep these checklists in a separate binder so they are easily referenced.

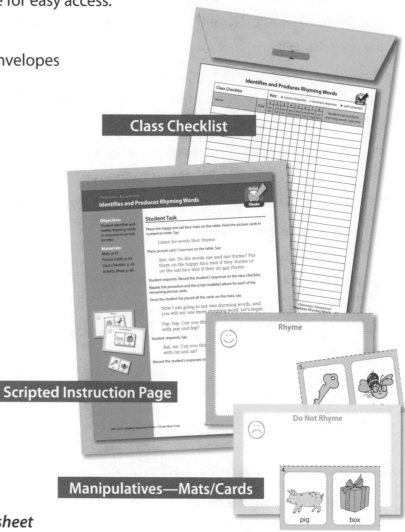

**Class Checklist**

**Scripted Instruction Page**

**Manipulatives—Mats/Cards**

**Activity Sheet**

# How to Conduct an Assessment

- **Be prepared.**

  Preread the scripted instructions. Follow the directions at the top of the script for setting out the cards and mats. Have the class checklist at hand to record the student's responses. Do not ask the student to come to the table until all task materials are in place.

- **Provide a non-threatening atmosphere.**

  The student should complete the task at a quiet, isolated table. Refer to the activity as a "task" or "job," not as a "test."

- **Provide a non-distracting environment.**

  The student should be able to easily focus on the task. Sit next to the student. Communicate in a clear, concise way.

- **Be an unbiased assessor.**

  Do not encourage or discourage or approve or disapprove of the student's responses. Be careful not to use facial expressions that provide feedback.

- **Know when to stop the assessment.**

  Discontinue the assessment activity if it becomes obvious that the student cannot do the task.

- **Be discreet.**

  When recording the student's responses, keep the checklist close to you so it will not distract the student.

---

## What does this mean?

/p/   When a letter is between / /, the letter sound, not the letter name, should be pronounced.

c•at   When a bullet appears within a word, emphasize each word part separately.

(˘)   is used to represent short vowel sounds: căt, gĕt, ĭt, hŏt, pŭp.

(¯)   is used to represent long vowel sounds: cāke, mē, bīte, hōme, ūse.

Auditory
Only
   Some tasks are auditory only, and are indicated by this icon on the teacher script page. Auditory tasks do not contain mats or task cards.

---

# Individual Student Assessment Checklist

Name _____     School Year _____

| Skill | Dates Tested | Date Mastered |
|---|---|---|
| **Unit 1—Phonemic Awareness** | | |
| Initial, Medial Vowel, and Final Sound Substitution | | |
| Initial and Final Sound Deletion | | |
| Deletes Initial Phoneme in a Blend; Deletes Final Phoneme in a Blend | | |
| **Unit 2—Phonics and Word Recognition** | | |
| Discriminates and Identifies Digraphs: *sh, wh, th, ch* | | |
| Discriminates Long Vowel Spelling Patterns | | |
| Uses Diphthong Spelling Patterns: *oi, oy, ou, ow* | | |
| Segments Multisyllabic Words | | |
| Forms and Reads Regular Plurals | | |
| Reads Irregular Plurals | | |
| Identifies Abbreviations | | |
| Distinguishes Between Consonant Blends: *cr, fr, gr, dr, tr, br* | | |
| Distinguishes Between Consonant Blends: *sl, sk, sm, st, sp, sw* | | |
| Distinguishes Between Consonant Blends: *bl, cl, fl, gl, pl, sl* | | |
| Identifies and Reads Word Families | | |
| **Unit 3—Vocabulary and Concept Development** | | |
| Reads and Understands Antonyms | | |
| Reads and Understands Synonyms | | |
| Matches Words with Prefixes | | |
| Matches Words with Suffixes | | |
| Uses Multiple-Meaning Words | | |
| **Unit 4—Reading Comprehension** | | |
| Understands Cause and Effect | | |
| Follows Written Multiple-Step Directions | | |
| Understands Sequence of Events | | |

# Correlation Chart

School Year _____

| Skill | Week | Lesson |
|---|---|---|
| **Unit 1—Phonemic Awareness** | | |
| Initial, Medial Vowel, and Final Sound Substitution | | |
| Initial and Final Sound Deletion | | |
| Deletes Initial Phoneme in a Blend; Deletes Final Phoneme in a Blend | | |
| **Unit 2—Phonics and Word Recognition** | | |
| Discriminates and Identifies Digraphs: *sh, wh, th, ch* | | |
| Discriminates Long Vowel Spelling Patterns | | |
| Uses Diphthong Spelling Patterns: *oi, oy, ou, ow* | | |
| Segments Multisyllabic Words | | |
| Forms and Reads Regular Plurals | | |
| Reads Irregular Plurals | | |
| Identifies Abbreviations | | |
| Distinguishes Between Consonant Blends: *cr, fr, gr, dr, tr, br* | | |
| Distinguishes Between Consonant Blends: *sl, sk, sm, st, sp, sw* | | |
| Distinguishes Between Consonant Blends: *bl, cl, fl, gl, pl, sl* | | |
| Identifies and Reads Word Families | | |
| **Unit 3—Vocabulary and Concept Development** | | |
| Reads and Understands Antonyms | | |
| Reads and Understands Synonyms | | |
| Matches Words with Prefixes | | |
| Matches Words with Suffixes | | |
| Uses Multiple-Meaning Words | | |
| **Unit 4—Reading Comprehension** | | |
| Understands Cause and Effect | | |
| Follows Written Multiple-Step Directions | | |
| Understands Sequence of Events | | |

**Quick Checks**

## Unit 1
# Phonemic Awareness

**Objective:**
Student substitutes initial, medial, and final sounds in orally stated words.

**Materials:**
Class Checklist, p. 11

Activity Sheet, p. 12

Auditory
Only

## Student Task

Say:

> Listen to the word I say and follow the directions I give you. Let's begin.

Initial sound. Say:

> Replace the first sound in *bite* with /k/.

Student responds. Record the student's response on the class checklist. Say:

> Replace the first sound in *tone* with /b/.

Record the student's response.

Medial vowel sound. Say:

> Replace the middle sound in *sit* with /a/.

Record the student's response. Say:

> Replace the middle sound in *net* with /o/.

Record the student's response.

Final sound. Say:

> Replace the final sound in *bed* with /t/.

Record the student's response. Say:

> Replace the final sound in *rat* with /n/.

Record the student's response.

# Initial, Medial Vowel, and Final Sound Substitution

| Class Checklist | | Key: | **+** correct response | **−** incorrect response | | **●** self-corrected | |
|---|---|---|---|---|---|---|---|

| Name | Date | Initial /k/:kite | Initial /b/:bone | Medial /a/:sat | Medial /o/:not | Final /t/:bet | Final /n/:ran | Notes |
|---|---|---|---|---|---|---|---|---|
| | | | | | | | | |
| | | | | | | | | |
| | | | | | | | | |
| | | | | | | | | |
| | | | | | | | | |
| | | | | | | | | |
| | | | | | | | | |
| | | | | | | | | |
| | | | | | | | | |
| | | | | | | | | |
| | | | | | | | | |
| | | | | | | | | |
| | | | | | | | | |
| | | | | | | | | |
| | | | | | | | | |
| | | | | | | | | |
| | | | | | | | | |
| | | | | | | | | |
| | | | | | | | | |
| | | | | | | | | |
| | | | | | | | | |
| | | | | | | | | |
| | | | | | | | | |

**Phonemic Awareness**
Initial, Medial Vowel, and Final Sound Substitution

Name _____

**Activity Sheet**

# What Do You Hear?

Name each picture. Listen for the beginning sound.
Circle the letter you hear.

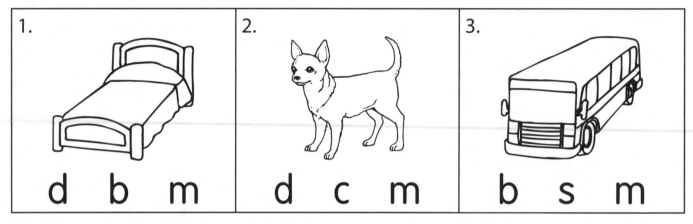

| 1. | 2. | 3. |
|---|---|---|
| d  b  m | d  c  m | b  s  m |

Name each picture. Listen for the middle sound.
Circle the letter you hear.

| 4. | 5. | 6. |
|---|---|---|
| i  o  e | a  e  u | a  i  e |

Name each picture. Listen for the ending sound.
Circle the letter you hear.

| 7. | 8. | 9. |
|---|---|---|
| f  c  t | s  p  l | g  d  t |

EMC 3339 • Reading Assessment Tasks • © Evan-Moor Corp.

## Objective:

Student orally identifies the initial and final sounds of a given set of words.

## Materials:

Class Checklist, p. 15

Activity Sheet, p. 16

**Auditory Only**

## Student Task

Say:

> Listen to the word I say and follow the directions I give you. Let's begin.

Initial sound. Say:

> Say *gate* without the /g/.

Student responds. Record the student's response on the class checklist. Say:

> Say *bean* without the /b/.

Record the student's response.

Final sound. Say:

> Say *mug* without the /g/.

Record the student's response. Say:

> Say *beef* without the /f/.

Record the student's response.

# Initial and Final Sound Deletion

| Class Checklist | | Key: + correct response — incorrect response ● self-corrected | | | | |
|---|---|---|---|---|---|---|
| Name | Date | Deletes /g/ in *gate* | Deletes /b/ in *bean* | Deletes /g/ in *mug* | Deletes /f/ in *beef* | Notes |
| | | | | | | |
| | | | | | | |
| | | | | | | |
| | | | | | | |
| | | | | | | |
| | | | | | | |
| | | | | | | |
| | | | | | | |
| | | | | | | |
| | | | | | | |
| | | | | | | |
| | | | | | | |
| | | | | | | |
| | | | | | | |
| | | | | | | |
| | | | | | | |
| | | | | | | |
| | | | | | | |
| | | | | | | |
| | | | | | | |
| | | | | | | |
| | | | | | | |
| | | | | | | |
| | | | | | | |

Name _____

# Beginning and Ending Sound

Name each picture.
Listen for the beginning sound. Write the letter.

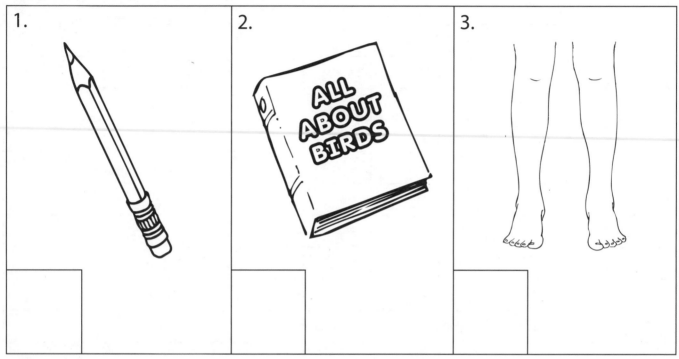

Name each picture.
Listen for the ending sound. Write the letter.

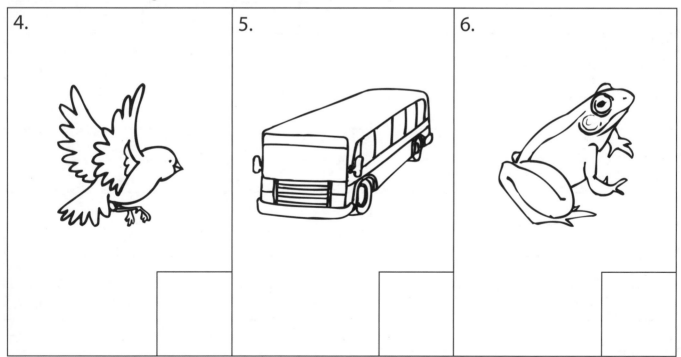

**Objective:**
Student deletes the initial phoneme in a blend. Student deletes the final phoneme in a blend.

**Materials:**
Class Checklist, p. 19
Activity Sheet, p. 20

**Auditory Only**

## Student Task

Initial blend. Say:

> Listen to the word I say and follow the directions I give you. Let's begin.
>
> Say *step* without the /s/.

Student responds. Record the student's response on the class checklist. Say:

> Say *plate* without the /p/.

Record the student's response. Say:

> Say *frog* without the /f/.

Record the student's response.

Final blend. Say:

> Say *west* without the /t/.

Record the student's response. Say:

> Say *lump* without the /p/.

Record the student's response. Say:

> Say *cart* without the /t/.

Record the student's response.

EMC 3339 • Reading Assessment Tasks • © Evan-Moor Corp.

**Phonemic Awareness**
Deletes Initial Phoneme in a Blend;
Deletes Final Phoneme in a Blend　**17**

# Deletes Initial Phoneme in a Blend;
# Deletes Final Phoneme in a Blend

| Class Checklist | | Key: + correct response  − incorrect response  • self-corrected | | | | | |
|---|---|---|---|---|---|---|---|
| Name | Date | Deletes /s/ in step | Deletes /p/ in plate | Deletes /f/ in frog | Deletes /t/ in west | Deletes /p/ in lump | Deletes /t/ in cart |
| | | | | | | | |
| | | | | | | | |
| | | | | | | | |
| | | | | | | | |
| | | | | | | | |
| | | | | | | | |
| | | | | | | | |
| | | | | | | | |
| | | | | | | | |
| | | | | | | | |
| | | | | | | | |
| | | | | | | | |
| | | | | | | | |
| | | | | | | | |
| | | | | | | | |
| | | | | | | | |
| | | | | | | | |
| | | | | | | | |
| | | | | | | | |
| | | | | | | | |
| | | | | | | | |
| | | | | | | | |
| | | | | | | | |
| | | | | | | | |

**Phonemic Awareness**
Deletes Initial Phoneme in a Blend;
Deletes Final Phoneme in a Blend

Name _____

# Beginning and Ending Sounds

Name each picture. Write the missing letter.

| | |
|---|---|
| 1. ___oat | 2. ___nail |
| 3. fro___ | 4. ves___ |
| 5. lam___ | 6. ___est |

**Phonemic Awareness**
Deletes Initial Phoneme in a Blend;
**20** Deletes Final Phoneme in a Blend

EMC 3339 • Reading Assessment Tasks • © Evan-Moor Corp.

**Quick Checks**

## Unit 2
# Phonics and Word Recognition

# Discriminates and Identifies Digraphs: *sh, wh, th, ch*

**Objective:**

Student listens to a word with a beginning or an ending digraph and identifies each digraph.

**Materials:**

Mat, p. 25

Digraph Cards, p. 25

Class Checklist, p. 27

Activity Sheet, p. 28

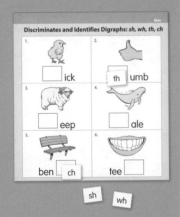

## Student Task

Place the mat on the table. Lay the digraph cards faceup on the table. Say:

> Listen to the beginning sound in each word. Then choose the letters that make the beginning sound. Let's begin.

Point to box 1. Say:

> *Chick.* Choose the letters that make the /ch/ sound. Place them on the mat.

Student responds. Point to box 2. Say:

> *Thumb.* Choose the letters that make the /th/ sound.

Student responds. Point to box 3. Say:

> *Sheep.* Choose the letters that make the /sh/ sound.

Student responds. Point to box 4. Say:

> *Whale.* Choose the letters that make the /wh/ sound.

Student responds. Say:

> Now you will listen to the *ending* sound in each word. Let's begin.

Point to box 5. Say:

> *Bench.* Choose the letters that make the /ch/ sound. Place them on the mat.

Student responds. Point to box 6. Say:

> *Teeth.* Choose the letters that make the /th/ sound.

Student responds. Use the mat to record the student's responses on the class checklist.

Phonics and Word Recognition
Discriminates and Identifies Digraphs: *sh, wh, th, ch*

# Discriminates and Identifies Digraphs: *sh, wh, th, ch*

1. ☐ ick

2. ☐ umb

3. ☐ eep

4. ☐ ale

5. ben ☐

6. tee ☐

| th | ch | th | sh | ch | wh | th |
|----|----|----|----|----|----|----|

**Discriminates and Identifies Digraphs:** *sh, wh, th, ch*

Phonics and Word Recognition

EMC 3339 • © Evan-Moor Corp.

| Digraphs:<br>*sh, wh, th, ch*<br>Phonics and Word<br>Recognition<br><br>EMC 3339<br>© Evan-Moor Corp. | Digraphs:<br>*sh, wh, th, ch*<br>Phonics and Word<br>Recognition<br><br>EMC 3339<br>© Evan-Moor Corp. | Digraphs:<br>*sh, wh, th, ch*<br>Phonics and Word<br>Recognition<br><br>EMC 3339<br>© Evan-Moor Corp. | Digraphs:<br>*sh, wh, th, ch*<br>Phonics and Word<br>Recognition<br><br>EMC 3339<br>© Evan-Moor Corp. | Digraphs:<br>*sh, wh, th, ch*<br>Phonics and Word<br>Recognition<br><br>EMC 3339<br>© Evan-Moor Corp. | Digraphs:<br>*sh, wh, th, ch*<br>Phonics and Word<br>Recognition<br><br>EMC 3339<br>© Evan-Moor Corp. | Digraphs:<br>*sh, wh, th, ch*<br>Phonics and Word<br>Recognition<br><br>EMC 3339<br>© Evan-Moor Corp. |
|---|---|---|---|---|---|---|

**Phonics and Word Recognition**

**26** Discriminates and Identifies Digraphs: *sh, wh, th, ch*    EMC 3339 • Reading Assessment Tasks • © Evan-Moor Corp.

# Discriminates and Identifies Digraphs: *sh, wh, th, ch*

| Class Checklist | | Key: + correct response  − incorrect response  • self-corrected | | | | | | |
|---|---|---|---|---|---|---|---|---|
| Name | Date | chick ch | thumb th | sheep sh | whale wh | bench ch | teeth th | Notes |
| | | | | | | | | |
| | | | | | | | | |
| | | | | | | | | |
| | | | | | | | | |
| | | | | | | | | |
| | | | | | | | | |
| | | | | | | | | |
| | | | | | | | | |
| | | | | | | | | |
| | | | | | | | | |
| | | | | | | | | |
| | | | | | | | | |
| | | | | | | | | |
| | | | | | | | | |
| | | | | | | | | |
| | | | | | | | | |
| | | | | | | | | |
| | | | | | | | | |
| | | | | | | | | |
| | | | | | | | | |
| | | | | | | | | |
| | | | | | | | | |
| | | | | | | | | |

**Phonics and Word Recognition**

Name _____

# sh, wh, th, ch

Name each picture.
Listen for the beginning sound.
Write the letters that make the beginning sound.

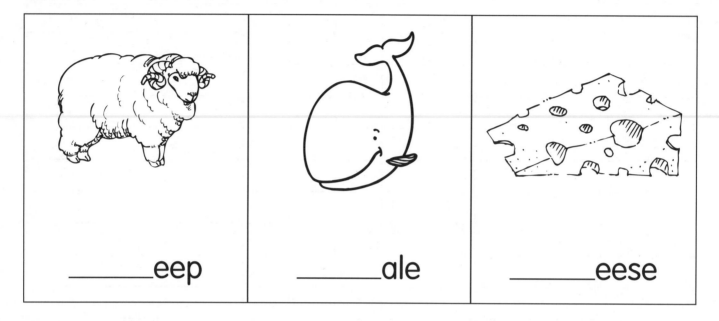

_____eep          _____ale          _____eese

Name each picture.
Listen for the ending sound.
Write the letters that make the ending sound.

ben_____          fi_____          tee_____

# Discriminates Long Vowel Spelling Patterns

**Quick**
**Checks**

## Objective:

Student discriminates long vowel spelling patterns (long vowel digraphs) in words.

## Materials:

Mat, p. 31

Picture Cards, p. 33

Class Checklist, p. 35

Activity Sheet, p. 36

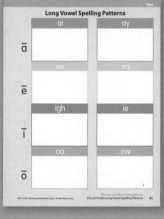

## Student Task

Place the mat on the table. Place the picture cards faceup in random order. Say:

> Long vowels have different spelling patterns. Today we will look at a few of the spelling patterns.

Point the green row on the mat. Say:

> *ai* makes the /ā/ sound and *ay* makes the /ā/ sound. Both spellings make the /ā/ sound.

Point to the yellow row on the mat. Say:

> *ee* makes the /ē/ sound and *ea* makes the /ē/ sound. Both spellings make the /ē/ sound.

Point to the blue row on the mat. Say:

> *igh* makes the /ī/ sound and *ie* makes the /ī/ sound. Both spellings make the /ī/ sound.

Point to the orange row on the mat. Say:

> *oa* makes the /ō/ sound and *ow* makes the /ō/ sound. Both spellings make the /ō/ sound.
>
> Now look at the picture cards. Each picture card belongs in a box under a long vowel spelling pattern. Let's do the first one together.

Point to the snail picture card. Point to the long *a* boxes on the mat. Say:

> *Snail.* Which long vowel spelling pattern is in the word *snail*? *ai* or *ay*? Place the card in the box under the correct spelling pattern.

Student responds. Say:

> Now choose another picture card and put it in the box under the correct spelling pattern.

Student responds. The student continues placing the picture cards at his or her own pace. Once the student has placed all the picture cards, use the mat to record the student's responses on the class checklist.

# Long Vowel Spelling Patterns

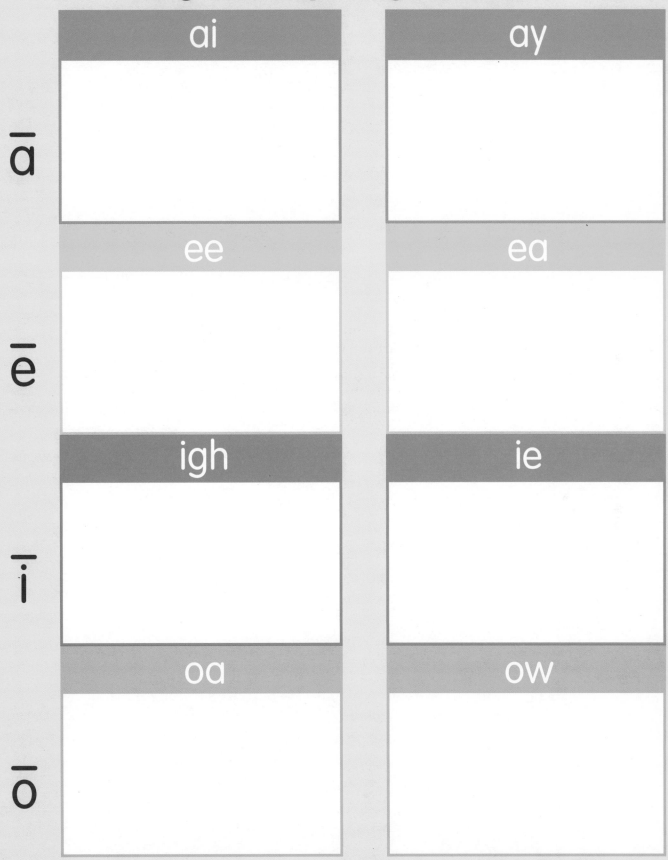

**Phonics and Word Recognition**
Discriminates Long Vowel Spelling Patterns

# Discriminates Long Vowel Spelling Patterns

## Phonics and Word Recognition

EMC 3339 • © Evan-Moor Corp.

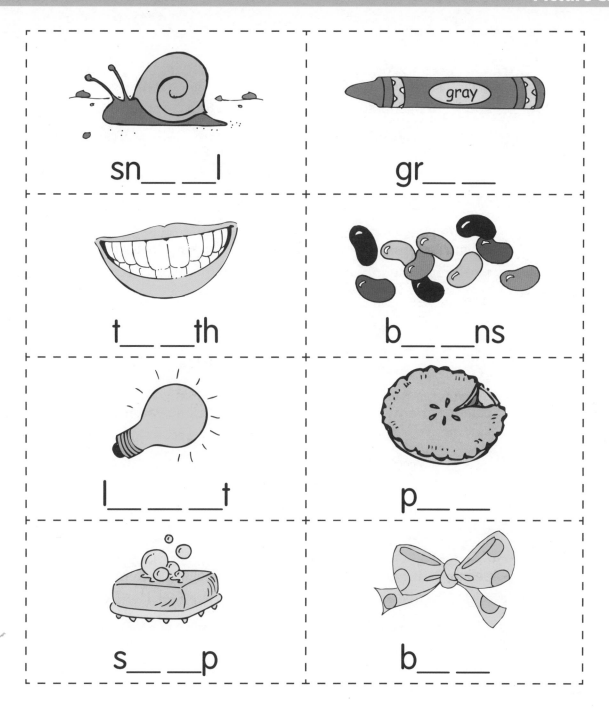

sn__ __l

gr__ __

t__ __th

b__ __ns

l__ __ __t

p__ __

s__ __p

b__ __

**Phonics and Word Recognition**
Discriminates Long Vowel Spelling Patterns **33**

**Discriminates Long Vowel
Spelling Patterns**

Phonics and Word Recognition

EMC 3339 • © Evan-Moor Corp.

**Discriminates Long Vowel
Spelling Patterns**

Phonics and Word Recognition

EMC 3339 • © Evan-Moor Corp.

**Discriminates Long Vowel
Spelling Patterns**

Phonics and Word Recognition

EMC 3339 • © Evan-Moor Corp.

**Discriminates Long Vowel
Spelling Patterns**

Phonics and Word Recognition

EMC 3339 • © Evan-Moor Corp.

**Discriminates Long Vowel
Spelling Patterns**

Phonics and Word Recognition

EMC 3339 • © Evan-Moor Corp.

**Discriminates Long Vowel
Spelling Patterns**

Phonics and Word Recognition

EMC 3339 • © Evan-Moor Corp.

**Discriminates Long Vowel
Spelling Patterns**

Phonics and Word Recognition

EMC 3339 • © Evan-Moor Corp.

**Discriminates Long Vowel
Spelling Patterns**

Phonics and Word Recognition

EMC 3339 • © Evan-Moor Corp.

# Discriminates Long Vowel Spelling Patterns

| Class Checklist | | Key: + correct response  − incorrect response  ● self-corrected | | | | | | | |
|---|---|---|---|---|---|---|---|---|---|
| Name | Date | snail<br>ai | gray<br>ay | teeth<br>ee | beans<br>ea | light<br>igh | pie<br>ie | soap<br>oa | bow<br>ow |
| | | | | | | | | | |
| | | | | | | | | | |
| | | | | | | | | | |
| | | | | | | | | | |
| | | | | | | | | | |
| | | | | | | | | | |
| | | | | | | | | | |
| | | | | | | | | | |
| | | | | | | | | | |
| | | | | | | | | | |
| | | | | | | | | | |
| | | | | | | | | | |
| | | | | | | | | | |
| | | | | | | | | | |
| | | | | | | | | | |
| | | | | | | | | | |
| | | | | | | | | | |
| | | | | | | | | | |
| | | | | | | | | | |
| | | | | | | | | | |
| | | | | | | | | | |
| | | | | | | | | | |
| | | | | | | | | | |
| | | | | | | | | | |

Name _____

# Which Pattern?

Write the long vowel spelling pattern to finish spelling each word.

| ai | ay | ee | ea | igh | ie | oa | ow |
|----|----|----|----|-----|----|----|----|

1.

tr __ __ n

2.

s __ __ p

3.

t __ __

4.

l __ __ t

5.

tr __ __

6.

t __ __

# Uses Diphthong Spelling Patterns: *oi, oy, ou, ow*

Quick
Checks

## Objective:

Student uses diphthong spelling patterns *oi, oy, ou,* and *ow*.

## Materials:

Mat 1, p. 39

Mat 2, p. 41

Yellow Picture Cards, p. 39

Green Picture Cards, p. 41

Class Checklist, p. 43

Activity Sheet, p. 44

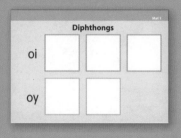

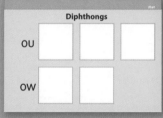

## Student Task

Place mat 1 on the table. Place the yellow picture cards faceup in a row. Point to the mat. Pronounce the /oy/ sound as in *coin*. Say:

> The vowel pairs *oi* and *oy* stand for the /oy/ sound.

Place the coin picture card in front of the student. Say:

> This picture shows coins. Is *coin* spelled with *oi* or *oy*? Place the picture card in the box on the mat next to *oi* or *oy*.

Student responds. Say:

> Now look at the rest of the picture cards and place them next to *oi* or *oy* on the mat.

Student places the picture cards on the mat at his or her own pace. Use the mat to record the student's responses on the class checklist.

Remove the mat and cards from the table. Then place mat 2 on the table. Place the green picture cards faceup in a row. Point to the mat. Pronounce the /ow/ sound as in *cow*. Say:

> Now let's look at the vowel pairs *ou* and *ow*. *Ou* and *ow* stand for the /ow/ sound.

Place the cow picture card in front of the student. Say:

> This picture shows a cow. Is *cow* spelled with *ou* or *ow*? Place the picture card in the box on the mat next to *ou* or *ow*.

Student responds. Say:

> Now look at the rest of the picture cards and place them next to *ou* or *ow* on the mat.

Student places the picture cards on the mat at his or her own pace. Use the mat to record the student's responses on the class checklist.

# Diphthongs

oi

oy

c _____ n        s _____ l        b _____

_____ l        t _____

**Phonics and Word Recognition**
Uses Diphthong Spelling Patterns: *oi, oy, ou, ow*        **39**

**Uses Diphthong Spelling Patterns:** *oi, oy, ou, ow*

Phonics and Word Recognition

EMC 3339 • © Evan-Moor Corp.

**Uses
Diphthong
Spelling
Patterns:**
*oi, oy, ou, ow*

Phonics and Word
Recognition

EMC 3339 • © Evan-Moor Corp.

**Uses
Diphthong
Spelling
Patterns:**
*oi, oy, ou, ow*

Phonics and Word
Recognition

EMC 3339 • © Evan-Moor Corp.

**Uses
Diphthong
Spelling
Patterns:**
*oi, oy, ou, ow*

Phonics and Word
Recognition

EMC 3339 • © Evan-Moor Corp.

**Uses
Diphthong
Spelling
Patterns:**
*oi, oy, ou, ow*

Phonics and Word
Recognition

EMC 3339 • © Evan-Moor Corp.

**Uses
Diphthong
Spelling
Patterns:**
*oi, oy, ou, ow*

Phonics and Word
Recognition

EMC 3339 • © Evan-Moor Corp.

# Diphthongs

OU

OW

c ___ ___

h ___ ___ se

m ___ ___ se

cl___ ___ n

m___ ___ th

**Phonics and Word Recognition**
Uses Diphthong Spelling Patterns: *oi, oy, ou, ow*   **41**

**Uses Diphthong Spelling Patterns:** *oi, oy, ou, ow*

Phonics and Word Recognition

EMC 3339 • © Evan-Moor Corp.

**Uses Diphthong Spelling Patterns:** *oi, oy, ou, ow*

Phonics and Word Recognition

EMC 3339 • © Evan-Moor Corp.

**Uses Diphthong Spelling Patterns:** *oi, oy, ou, ow*

Phonics and Word Recognition

EMC 3339 • © Evan-Moor Corp.

**Uses Diphthong Spelling Patterns:** *oi, oy, ou, ow*

Phonics and Word Recognition

EMC 3339 • © Evan-Moor Corp.

**Uses Diphthong Spelling Patterns:** *oi, oy, ou, ow*

Phonics and Word Recognition

EMC 3339 • © Evan-Moor Corp.

**Uses Diphthong Spelling Patterns:** *oi, oy, ou, ow*

Phonics and Word Recognition

EMC 3339 • © Evan-Moor Corp.

# Uses Diphthong Spelling Patterns: *oi, oy, ou, ow*

| Class Checklist | | Key: | + correct response | — incorrect response | • self-corrected | | | | | |
|---|---|---|---|---|---|---|---|---|---|---|
| Name | Date | coin oi | soil oi | oil oi | boy oy | toy oy | house ou | mouse ou | mouth ou | cow ow | clown ow | Notes |
| | | | | | | | | | | | |
| | | | | | | | | | | | |
| | | | | | | | | | | | |
| | | | | | | | | | | | |
| | | | | | | | | | | | |
| | | | | | | | | | | | |
| | | | | | | | | | | | |
| | | | | | | | | | | | |
| | | | | | | | | | | | |
| | | | | | | | | | | | |
| | | | | | | | | | | | |
| | | | | | | | | | | | |
| | | | | | | | | | | | |
| | | | | | | | | | | | |
| | | | | | | | | | | | |
| | | | | | | | | | | | |
| | | | | | | | | | | | |
| | | | | | | | | | | | |
| | | | | | | | | | | | |
| | | | | | | | | | | | |
| | | | | | | | | | | | |
| | | | | | | | | | | | |
| | | | | | | | | | | | |
| | | | | | | | | | | | |

Note: Student writes the correct diphthong to finish spelling each word.

Name _____

# Missing Letters

Write the missing letters to name each picture.

| oi    oy    ou    ow |

**1.**

h __ __ se

**2.**

m __ __ se

**3.**

c __ __

**4.**

__ __ l

**5.**

c __ __ ns

**6.**

t __ __ s

# Segments Multisyllabic Words

**Objective:**
Student segments multisyllabic words.

**Materials:**
Green Word Cards, p. 47
Orange Word Cards, p. 49
Class Checklist, p. 51
Activity Sheet, p. 52

**Setup:**
You must laminate the word cards for this task. Students will use a wipe-off marker to segment the words.

## Model the Task

Place the green word cards faceup in a row on the table. Choose the *candy* card. Say:

> Today we are going to divide words into syllables. I am going to divide the word *candy* into syllables.

Draw a line between the *n* and the *d* with a wipe-off marker. Say:

> can•dy

## Student Task

> Now it's your turn. Choose a card. Read me the word and draw a line to divide the word into syllables. Let's begin.

> Choose a card and read the word to me.

Student responds. Say:

> Now draw a line to divide the word into syllables.

Student responds. Say:

> Choose another card, read the word to me, and draw a line to divide the word into syllables.

Student responds. Record the student's responses on the class checklist. You may wish to use the orange word cards to extend the assessment or for retesting purposes.

**Syllable division key**

| Green word cards: | | Orange word cards: | |
|---|---|---|---|
| ta/ble | kit/ten | hab/it | lim/it |
| di/ver | ten/nis | sig/nal | ba/sic |
| be/fore | rab/bit | co/zy | so/lo |
| po/ny | can/dy | | |

table

diver

before

pony

kitten

tennis

rabbit

candy

**Segments Multisyllabic Words**

Phonics and Word Recognition

EMC 3339 • © Evan-Moor Corp.

**Segments Multisyllabic Words**

Phonics and Word Recognition

EMC 3339 • © Evan-Moor Corp.

**Segments Multisyllabic Words**

Phonics and Word Recognition

EMC 3339 • © Evan-Moor Corp.

**Segments Multisyllabic Words**

Phonics and Word Recognition

EMC 3339 • © Evan-Moor Corp.

**Segments Multisyllabic Words**

Phonics and Word Recognition

EMC 3339 • © Evan-Moor Corp.

**Segments Multisyllabic Words**

Phonics and Word Recognition

EMC 3339 • © Evan-Moor Corp.

**Segments Multisyllabic Words**

Phonics and Word Recognition

EMC 3339 • © Evan-Moor Corp.

**Segments Multisyllabic Words**

Phonics and Word Recognition

EMC 3339 • © Evan-Moor Corp.

habit

signal

cozy

limit

basic

solo

**Phonics and Word Recognition**
Segments Multisyllabic Words    **49**

**Segments Multisyllabic Words**

Phonics and Word Recognition

EMC 3339 • © Evan-Moor Corp.

**Segments Multisyllabic Words**

Phonics and Word Recognition

EMC 3339 • © Evan-Moor Corp.

**Segments Multisyllabic Words**

Phonics and Word Recognition

EMC 3339 • © Evan-Moor Corp.

**Segments Multisyllabic Words**

Phonics and Word Recognition

EMC 3339 • © Evan-Moor Corp.

**Segments Multisyllabic Words**

Phonics and Word Recognition

EMC 3339 • © Evan-Moor Corp.

**Segments Multisyllabic Words**

Phonics and Word Recognition

EMC 3339 • © Evan-Moor Corp.

# Segments Multisyllabic Words

| Class Checklist | | Record any words the student incorrectly segmented below. |
|---|---|---|
| Name | Date | Incorrectly Segmented Words |
| | | |
| | | |
| | | |
| | | |
| | | |
| | | |
| | | |
| | | |
| | | |
| | | |
| | | |
| | | |
| | | |
| | | |
| | | |
| | | |
| | | |
| | | |
| | | |
| | | |
| | | |
| | | |
| | | |

Note: Student segments multisyllabic words.

Name _____

# Divide Them Up

Draw a line to divide each word into syllables.

1. **coffee**

2. **tiger**

3. **sister**

4. **silly**

5. **cozy**

6. **penny**

7. **party**

8. **bonus**

9. **rodent**

10. **basket**

11. **label**

12. **swimming**

13. **platter**

14. **odor**

15. **mistake**

16. **table**

**Phonics and Word Recognition**
Segments Multisyllabic Words

# Forms and Reads Regular Plurals

**Objective:**
Student forms and reads regular plurals.

**Materials:**
Mat, p. 55

Plural Ending Cards, p. 55

Class Checklist, p. 57

Activity Sheet, p. 58

## Model the Task

Place the mat on the table. Place the plural ending cards faceup in rows. Say:

> Today we are going to add the correct ending to each word to make it plural.

> The first word says *plant*.

Place an *s* card next to the word *plant* to make it plural. Say:

> I add *s* to make it plural. Now it says *plants*.

## Student Task

> Now it's your turn. Read the next word on the mat to me. Add *s*, *es*, or *ies* to make it plural.

Student responds by placing a plural ending card next to the word on the mat. Say:

> Now read the word to me.

Student responds. Record the student's response on the class checklist. Say:

> Read the next word to me and add *s*, *es*, or *ies* to make it plural.

Student responds. Say:

> Now read the word to me.

Student responds. Record the student's response on the class checklist.

Repeat the procedure and the script modeled above for each of the remaining words on the mat.

.

# Forms and Reads Regular Plurals

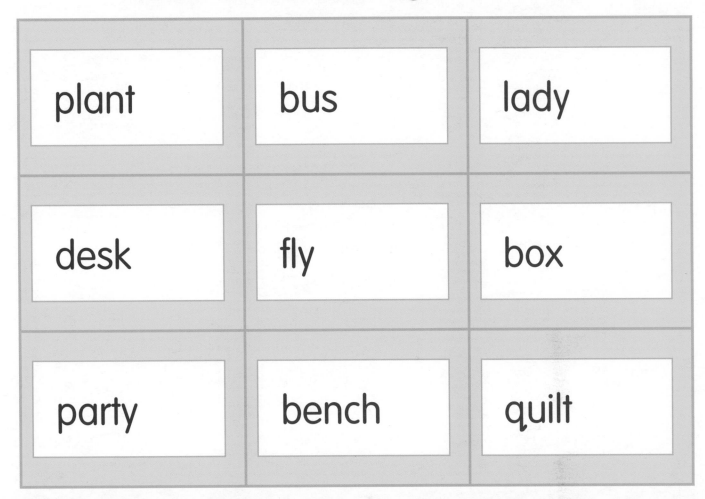

| | | |
|---|---|---|
| plant | bus | lady |
| desk | fly | box |
| party | bench | quilt |

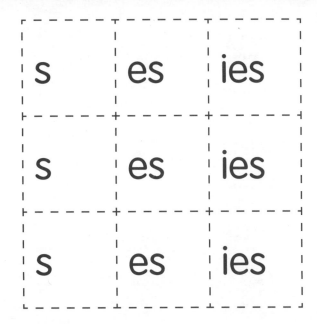

| | | |
|---|---|---|
| s | es | ies |
| s | es | ies |
| s | es | ies |

## Forms and Reads Regular Plurals

**Phonics and Word Recognition**

EMC 3339 • © Evan-Moor Corp.

**Forms and Reads
Regular Plurals**
Phonics and Word
Recognition

EMC 3339
© Evan-Moor Corp.

**Forms and Reads
Regular Plurals**
Phonics and Word
Recognition

EMC 3339
© Evan-Moor Corp.

**Forms and Reads
Regular Plurals**
Phonics and Word
Recognition

EMC 3339
© Evan-Moor Corp.

**Forms and Reads
Regular Plurals**
Phonics and Word
Recognition

EMC 3339
© Evan-Moor Corp.

**Forms and Reads
Regular Plurals**
Phonics and Word
Recognition

EMC 3339
© Evan-Moor Corp.

**Forms and Reads
Regular Plurals**
Phonics and Word
Recognition

EMC 3339
© Evan-Moor Corp.

**Forms and Reads
Regular Plurals**
Phonics and Word
Recognition

EMC 3339
© Evan-Moor Corp.

**Forms and Reads
Regular Plurals**
Phonics and Word
Recognition

EMC 3339
© Evan-Moor Corp.

**Forms and Reads
Regular Plurals**
Phonics and Word
Recognition

EMC 3339
© Evan-Moor Corp.

# Forms and Reads Regular Plurals

| Class Checklist | | Key: + correct response  − incorrect response  ● self-corrected | | | | | | | | | | |
|---|---|---|---|---|---|---|---|---|---|---|---|---|
| Name | Date | s plant | es bus | ies lady | s desk | ies fly | es box | ies party | es bench | s quilt | Notes |
| | | | | | | | | | | | |
| | | | | | | | | | | | |
| | | | | | | | | | | | |
| | | | | | | | | | | | |
| | | | | | | | | | | | |
| | | | | | | | | | | | |
| | | | | | | | | | | | |
| | | | | | | | | | | | |
| | | | | | | | | | | | |
| | | | | | | | | | | | |
| | | | | | | | | | | | |
| | | | | | | | | | | | |
| | | | | | | | | | | | |
| | | | | | | | | | | | |
| | | | | | | | | | | | |
| | | | | | | | | | | | |
| | | | | | | | | | | | |
| | | | | | | | | | | | |
| | | | | | | | | | | | |
| | | | | | | | | | | | |
| | | | | | | | | | | | |
| | | | | | | | | | | | |

**Phonics and Word Recognition**
Forms and Reads Regular Plurals

Note: Student circles the correct plural form in each row.

Name _____

# More Than One

Read the first word in each row.
Then circle the correct plural form.

| | | | |
|---|---|---|---|
| 1. chair | chaires | ⟨chairs⟩ | chairies |
| 2. pan | panes | panies | pans |
| 3. dish | dishs | dishes | dishies |
| 4. lady | ladys | ladyes | ladies |
| 5. dress | dresss | dresses | dressies |
| 6. inch | inches | inchs | inchies |
| 7. fox | foxs | foxes | foxies |
| 8. clock | clockies | clockes | clocks |

# Reads Irregular Plurals

**Objective:**
Student identifies and reads irregular plurals.

**Materials:**

Mat, p. 61

Word Cards, p. 63

Class Checklist, p. 65

Activity Sheet, p. 66

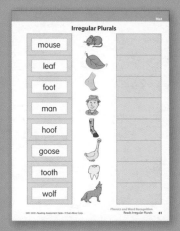

## Student Task

Place the mat on the table. Place the word cards faceup in rows on the table. Say:

> Today we are going to read a word and then find the plural. Let's begin.

Point to the word *mouse* on the mat. Say:

> Read this word to me.

Student responds. Say:

> Now find the card that names more than one mouse and place it on the mat.

Student responds. Say:

> Read the word to me.

Student responds. Point to the word *leaf* on the mat. Say:

> Read this word to me.

Student responds. Say:

> Now find the card that names more than one leaf and place it on the mat.

Student responds. Say:

> Read the word to me.

Repeat the procedures and the script modeled above for each of the remaining words on the mat. Use the mat as a reference to record the student's responses on the class checklist.

# Irregular Plurals

| mouse |
| leaf |
| foot |
| man |
| hoof |
| goose |
| tooth |
| wolf |

# Reads Irregular Plurals

**Phonics and Word Recognition**

EMC 3339 • © Evan-Moor Corp.

| | |
|---|---|
| mice | leaves |
| wolves | feet |
| men | hooves |
| geese | teeth |
| mans | mouses |
| tooths | footes |

**Phonics and Word Recognition**
Reads Irregular Plurals    **63**

**Reads Irregular Plurals**

Phonics and Word Recognition

EMC 3339 • © Evan-Moor Corp.

**Reads Irregular Plurals**

Phonics and Word Recognition

EMC 3339 • © Evan-Moor Corp.

**Reads Irregular Plurals**

Phonics and Word Recognition

EMC 3339 • © Evan-Moor Corp.

**Reads Irregular Plurals**

Phonics and Word Recognition

EMC 3339 • © Evan-Moor Corp.

**Reads Irregular Plurals**

Phonics and Word Recognition

EMC 3339 • © Evan-Moor Corp.

**Reads Irregular Plurals**

Phonics and Word Recognition

EMC 3339 • © Evan-Moor Corp.

**Reads Irregular Plurals**

Phonics and Word Recognition

EMC 3339 • © Evan-Moor Corp.

**Reads Irregular Plurals**

Phonics and Word Recognition

EMC 3339 • © Evan-Moor Corp.

**Reads Irregular Plurals**

Phonics and Word Recognition

EMC 3339 • © Evan-Moor Corp.

**Reads Irregular Plurals**

Phonics and Word Recognition

EMC 3339 • © Evan-Moor Corp.

**Reads Irregular Plurals**

Phonics and Word Recognition

EMC 3339 • © Evan-Moor Corp.

**Reads Irregular Plurals**

Phonics and Word Recognition

EMC 3339 • © Evan-Moor Corp.

# Reads Irregular Plurals

| Class Checklist | | Key: **+** correct response    **−** incorrect response    **●** self-corrected | | | | | | | | | |
|---|---|---|---|---|---|---|---|---|---|---|---|
| Name | Date | mouse mice | leaf leaves | foot feet | man men | hoof hooves | goose geese | tooth teeth | wolf wolves | Notes |
| | | | | | | | | | | |
| | | | | | | | | | | |
| | | | | | | | | | | |
| | | | | | | | | | | |
| | | | | | | | | | | |
| | | | | | | | | | | |
| | | | | | | | | | | |
| | | | | | | | | | | |
| | | | | | | | | | | |
| | | | | | | | | | | |
| | | | | | | | | | | |
| | | | | | | | | | | |
| | | | | | | | | | | |
| | | | | | | | | | | |
| | | | | | | | | | | |
| | | | | | | | | | | |
| | | | | | | | | | | |
| | | | | | | | | | | |
| | | | | | | | | | | |
| | | | | | | | | | | |
| | | | | | | | | | | |
| | | | | | | | | | | |
| | | | | | | | | | | |

Note: Student circles the correct plural form.

Name _____

# Two or More

Read the first word in each row.
Then circle the correct plural form.

| 1. wife | wifes | (wives) | wifies |
|---------|-------|---------|--------|
| 2. child | childes | childs | children |
| 3. foot | feet | footes | foots |
| 4. goose | gooses | geeses | geese |
| 5. man | mans | men | manes |
| 6. half | halfs | halfes | halves |
| 7. wolf | wolves | wolfes | wolfs |
| 8. tooth | teeth | toothes | tooths |

## Objective:
Student matches abbreviations to whole words.

## Materials:
Word and Abbreviation Cards, p. 69

Class Checklist, p. 71

Activity Sheet, p. 72

# Student Task

Place the word cards on the table faceup in a row in the following order: Doctor, Street, Mistress, February, Road, Monday, Avenue, Wednesday, miles per hour. Place the abbreviation cards on the table faceup in a row. Say:

> An abbreviation is a shorter way to write a word. Today we are going to read a word and match the word with its abbreviation. Let's begin.

Point to the word *Doctor*. Say:

> Read this word to me.

Student responds. Say:

> Now find its abbreviation and fit the cards together like a puzzle.

Student responds. Record the student's response on the class checklist. Point to the word *Street*. Say:

> Read this word to me.

Student responds. Say:

> Now find its abbreviation and fit the cards together like a puzzle.

Student responds. Record the student's response on the class checklist. Repeat the procedure and the script modeled above for each of the remaining word cards.

| | | |
|---|---|---|
| Dr. | St. | Mrs. |
| Doctor | Street | Mistress |
| Feb. | Rd. | Mon. |
| February | Road | Monday |
| Ave. | Wed. | mph |
| Avenue | Wednesday | miles per hour |

**Identifies Abbreviations**

Phonics and Word Recognition

EMC 3339 • © Evan-Moor Corp.

**Identifies Abbreviations**

Phonics and Word Recognition

EMC 3339 • © Evan-Moor Corp.

**Identifies Abbreviations**

Phonics and Word Recognition

EMC 3339 • © Evan-Moor Corp.

**Identifies Abbreviations**

Phonics and Word Recognition

EMC 3339 • © Evan-Moor Corp.

**Identifies Abbreviations**

Phonics and Word Recognition

EMC 3339 • © Evan-Moor Corp.

**Identifies Abbreviations**

Phonics and Word Recognition

EMC 3339 • © Evan-Moor Corp.

**Identifies Abbreviations**

Phonics and Word Recognition

EMC 3339 • © Evan-Moor Corp.

**Identifies Abbreviations**

Phonics and Word Recognition

EMC 3339 • © Evan-Moor Corp.

**Identifies Abbreviations**

Phonics and Word Recognition

EMC 3339 • © Evan-Moor Corp.

**Identifies Abbreviations**

Phonics and Word Recognition

EMC 3339 • © Evan-Moor Corp.

**Identifies Abbreviations**

Phonics and Word Recognition

EMC 3339 • © Evan-Moor Corp.

**Identifies Abbreviations**

Phonics and Word Recognition

EMC 3339 • © Evan-Moor Corp.

**Identifies Abbreviations**

Phonics and Word Recognition

EMC 3339 • © Evan-Moor Corp.

**Identifies Abbreviations**

Phonics and Word Recognition

EMC 3339 • © Evan-Moor Corp.

**Identifies Abbreviations**

Phonics and Word Recognition

EMC 3339 • © Evan-Moor Corp.

**Identifies Abbreviations**

Phonics and Word Recognition

EMC 3339 • © Evan-Moor Corp.

**Identifies Abbreviations**

Phonics and Word Recognition

EMC 3339 • © Evan-Moor Corp.

**Identifies Abbreviations**

Phonics and Word Recognition

EMC 3339 • © Evan-Moor Corp.

# Identifies Abbreviations

| Class Checklist | | Key: + correct response  − incorrect response  ● self-corrected | | | | | | | | |
|---|---|---|---|---|---|---|---|---|---|---|
| Name | Date | Doctor Dr. | Street St. | Mistress Mrs. | February Feb. | Road Rd. | Monday Mon. | Avenue Ave. | Wednesday Wed. | miles per hour mph |
| | | | | | | | | | | |
| | | | | | | | | | | |
| | | | | | | | | | | |
| | | | | | | | | | | |
| | | | | | | | | | | |
| | | | | | | | | | | |
| | | | | | | | | | | |
| | | | | | | | | | | |
| | | | | | | | | | | |
| | | | | | | | | | | |
| | | | | | | | | | | |
| | | | | | | | | | | |
| | | | | | | | | | | |
| | | | | | | | | | | |
| | | | | | | | | | | |
| | | | | | | | | | | |
| | | | | | | | | | | |
| | | | | | | | | | | |
| | | | | | | | | | | |
| | | | | | | | | | | |
| | | | | | | | | | | |
| | | | | | | | | | | |
| | | | | | | | | | | |

Name _____

# Shorten It

Read each word. Write the abbreviation.

| Dr. | Thurs. | Mr. | Jan. |
|-----|--------|-----|------|
| St. | Oct. | Tues. | |

1. Doctor _____

2. Tuesday _____

3. Mister _____

4. January _____

5. Street _____

6. Thursday _____

7. October _____

# Distinguishes Between Consonant Blends: *cr, fr, gr, dr, tr, br*

**Quick Checks**

**Objective:**
Student distinguishes consonant blends *cr, fr, gr, dr, tr,* and *br.*

**Materials:**
Mat, p. 75
Word Cards, p. 77
Class Checklist, p. 79
Activity Sheet, p. 80

## Model the Task

Place the mat on the table. Place the word cards faceup in a row on the table. Say:

> Look at the pictures on the mat. Listen to the beginning sounds as I say each picture name.

Point to each picture as you name it. Say:

> Crown, frog, grass, drum, truck, bread.

> Now look at the word cards. I will place a word card next to the picture with the same beginning sounds.

Place the *crack* word card on the mat in the first box next to the crown. Say:

> Crack. *Crack* begins with /cr/, so it belongs in the box next to the crown. Crack, crown. Both words begin with /cr/.

## Student Task

> Now it's your turn. Pick up a card and read the word to me.

Student responds. Say:

> Now place it in one of the boxes on the mat next to the picture with the same beginning sounds.

Student responds. Record the student's response on the class checklist. Say:

> Now choose another card and read the word to me.

Student responds. Say:

> Place the card in one of the boxes on the mat next to the picture with the same beginning sounds.

Record the student's response on the class checklist. Repeat the procedure and the script modeled above for each of the remaining word cards.

# Consonant Blends

| | | |
|---|---|---|
| 1. | | |
| 2. | | |
| 3. | | |
| 4. | | |
| 5. | | |
| 6. | | |

**Phonics and Word Recognition**
Distinguishes Between Consonant Blends:
*cr, fr, gr, dr, tr, br*    **75**

**Distinguishes Between Consonant Blends:**
*cr, fr, gr, dr, tr, br*

Phonics and Word Recognition

EMC 3339 • © Evan-Moor Corp.

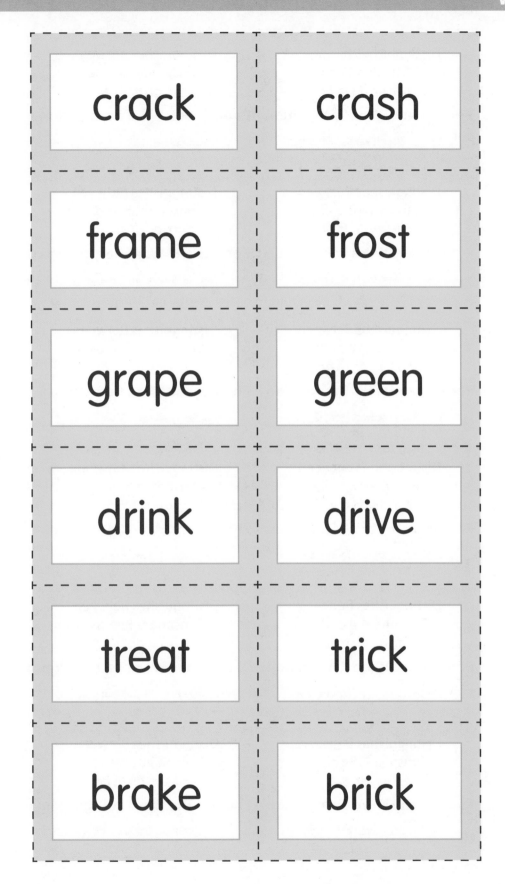

crack

crash

frame

frost

grape

green

drink

drive

treat

trick

brake

brick

**Phonics and Word Recognition**
Distinguishes Between Consonant Blends:
*cr, fr, gr, dr, tr, br*   **77**

**Distinguishes Between Consonant Blends:**
*cr, fr, gr, dr, tr, br*

Phonics and Word Recognition

EMC 3339 • © Evan-Moor Corp.

**Distinguishes Between Consonant Blends:**
*cr, fr, gr, dr, tr, br*

Phonics and Word Recognition

EMC 3339 • © Evan-Moor Corp.

**Distinguishes Between Consonant Blends:**
*cr, fr, gr, dr, tr, br*

Phonics and Word Recognition

EMC 3339 • © Evan-Moor Corp.

**Distinguishes Between Consonant Blends:**
*cr, fr, gr, dr, tr, br*

Phonics and Word Recognition

EMC 3339 • © Evan-Moor Corp.

**Distinguishes Between Consonant Blends:**
*cr, fr, gr, dr, tr, br*

Phonics and Word Recognition

EMC 3339 • © Evan-Moor Corp.

**Distinguishes Between Consonant Blends:**
*cr, fr, gr, dr, tr, br*

Phonics and Word Recognition

EMC 3339 • © Evan-Moor Corp.

**Distinguishes Between Consonant Blends:**
*cr, fr, gr, dr, tr, br*

Phonics and Word Recognition

EMC 3339 • © Evan-Moor Corp.

**Distinguishes Between Consonant Blends:**
*cr, fr, gr, dr, tr, br*

Phonics and Word Recognition

EMC 3339 • © Evan-Moor Corp.

**Distinguishes Between Consonant Blends:**
*cr, fr, gr, dr, tr, br*

Phonics and Word Recognition

EMC 3339 • © Evan-Moor Corp.

**Distinguishes Between Consonant Blends:**
*cr, fr, gr, dr, tr, br*

Phonics and Word Recognition

EMC 3339 • © Evan-Moor Corp.

**Distinguishes Between Consonant Blends:**
*cr, fr, gr, dr, tr, br*

Phonics and Word Recognition

EMC 3339 • © Evan-Moor Corp.

**Distinguishes Between Consonant Blends:**
*cr, fr, gr, dr, tr, br*

Phonics and Word Recognition

EMC 3339 • © Evan-Moor Corp.

# Distinguishes Between Consonant Blends: *cr, fr, gr, dr, tr, br*

| Class Checklist | | **Key:** + correct response | | – incorrect response | | | • self-corrected | |
|---|---|---|---|---|---|---|---|---|
| Name | Date | **cr:** crack crash | **fr:** frame frost | **gr:** grape green | **dr:** drink drive | **tr:** treat trick | **br:** brake brick | Notes |
| | | | | | | | | |
| | | | | | | | | |
| | | | | | | | | |
| | | | | | | | | |
| | | | | | | | | |
| | | | | | | | | |
| | | | | | | | | |
| | | | | | | | | |
| | | | | | | | | |
| | | | | | | | | |
| | | | | | | | | |
| | | | | | | | | |
| | | | | | | | | |
| | | | | | | | | |
| | | | | | | | | |
| | | | | | | | | |
| | | | | | | | | |
| | | | | | | | | |
| | | | | | | | | |
| | | | | | | | | |
| | | | | | | | | |

Note: Student says each picture name and writes a blend to complete each word.

Name ______________________

Activity Sheet

# Listen for Blends

Name each picture.
Listen to the sounds.
Write the missing letters.

| cr | fr | br | gr |
|---|---|---|---|

| | | |
|---|---|---|
| 1.  ___ ___ow | 2.  ___ ___og | 3.  ___ ___ame |
| 4.  ___ ___apes | 5.  ___ ___uit | 6.  ___ ___ay |
| 7.  ___ ___own | 8.  ___ ___ab | 9.  ___ ___ill |

Phonics and Word Recognition
Distinguishes Between Consonant Blends:
*cr, fr, gr, dr, tr, br*

# Distinguishes Between Consonant Blends: *sl, sk, sm, st, sp, sw*

**Quick Checks**

**Objective:**
Student distinguishes consonant blends *sl, sk, sm, st, sp,* and *sw*.

**Materials:**
Mat, p. 83
Word Cards, p. 85
Class Checklist, p. 87
Activity Sheet, p. 88

## Model the Task

Place the mat on the table. Place the word cards faceup in a row on the table. Say:

> Look at the pictures on the mat. Listen to the beginning sounds as I say each picture name.

Point to each picture as you name it. Say:

> Slide, skunk, smile, stamp, spoon, sweater.

> Now look at the word cards. I will place a word card next to the picture with the same beginning sounds.

Place the *slap* word card on the mat in the first box next to the slide. Say:

> Slap. *Slap* begins with /sl/, so it belongs in the box next to the slide. Slap, slide. Both words begin with /sl/.

## Student Task

> Now it's your turn. Pick up a card and read the word to me.

Student responds. Say:

> Now place it in one of the boxes on the mat next to the picture with the same beginning sounds.

Student responds. Record the student's response on the class checklist. Say:

> Now choose another card and read the word to me.

Student responds. Say:

> Place the card in one of the boxes on the mat next to the picture with the same beginning sounds.

Record the student's response on the class checklist. Repeat the procedure and the script modeled above for each of the remaining word cards.

**Phonics and Word Recognition**
Distinguishes Between Consonant Blends:
*sl, sk, sm, st, sp, sw*   **81**

# Consonant Blends

| | | |
|---|---|---|
| 1. | | |
| 2. | | |
| 3. | | |
| 4. | | |
| 5. | | |
| 6. | | |

**Phonics and Word Recognition**
Distinguishes Between Consonant Blends:
*sl, sk, sm, st, sp, sw*    **83**

**Distinguishes Between Consonant Blends:**
*sl, sk, sm, st, sp, sw*

Phonics and Word Recognition

EMC 3339 • © Evan-Moor Corp.

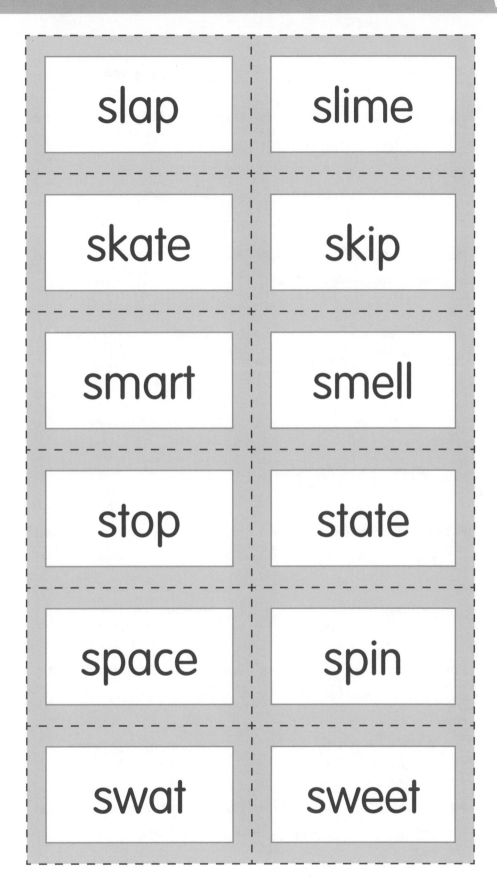

| | |
|---|---|
| slap | slime |
| skate | skip |
| smart | smell |
| stop | state |
| space | spin |
| swat | sweet |

**Phonics and Word Recognition**
Distinguishes Between Consonant Blends:
*sl, sk, sm, st, sp, sw*

**Distinguishes Between
Consonant Blends:**
*sl, sk, sm, st, sp, sw*

Phonics and Word Recognition

EMC 3339 • © Evan-Moor Corp.

**Distinguishes Between
Consonant Blends:**
*sl, sk, sm, st, sp, sw*

Phonics and Word Recognition

EMC 3339 • © Evan-Moor Corp.

**Distinguishes Between
Consonant Blends:**
*sl, sk, sm, st, sp, sw*

Phonics and Word Recognition

EMC 3339 • © Evan-Moor Corp.

**Distinguishes Between
Consonant Blends:**
*sl, sk, sm, st, sp, sw*

Phonics and Word Recognition

EMC 3339 • © Evan-Moor Corp.

**Distinguishes Between
Consonant Blends:**
*sl, sk, sm, st, sp, sw*

Phonics and Word Recognition

EMC 3339 • © Evan-Moor Corp.

**Distinguishes Between
Consonant Blends:**
*sl, sk, sm, st, sp, sw*

Phonics and Word Recognition

EMC 3339 • © Evan-Moor Corp.

**Distinguishes Between
Consonant Blends:**
*sl, sk, sm, st, sp, sw*

Phonics and Word Recognition

EMC 3339 • © Evan-Moor Corp.

**Distinguishes Between
Consonant Blends:**
*sl, sk, sm, st, sp, sw*

Phonics and Word Recognition

EMC 3339 • © Evan-Moor Corp.

**Distinguishes Between
Consonant Blends:**
*sl, sk, sm, st, sp, sw*

Phonics and Word Recognition

EMC 3339 • © Evan-Moor Corp.

**Distinguishes Between
Consonant Blends:**
*sl, sk, sm, st, sp, sw*

Phonics and Word Recognition

EMC 3339 • © Evan-Moor Corp.

**Distinguishes Between
Consonant Blends:**
*sl, sk, sm, st, sp, sw*

Phonics and Word Recognition

EMC 3339 • © Evan-Moor Corp.

**Distinguishes Between
Consonant Blends:**
*sl, sk, sm, st, sp, sw*

Phonics and Word Recognition

EMC 3339 • © Evan-Moor Corp.

# Distinguishes Between Consonant Blends: *sl, sk, sm, st, sp, sw*

| Class Checklist | | Key: + correct response  − incorrect response  ● self-corrected | | | | | | |
|---|---|---|---|---|---|---|---|---|
| Name | Date | sl:<br>slap<br>slime | sk:<br>skate<br>skip | sm:<br>smart<br>smell | st:<br>stop<br>state | sp:<br>space<br>spin | sw:<br>swat<br>sweet | Notes |
| | | | | | | | | |
| | | | | | | | | |
| | | | | | | | | |
| | | | | | | | | |
| | | | | | | | | |
| | | | | | | | | |
| | | | | | | | | |
| | | | | | | | | |
| | | | | | | | | |
| | | | | | | | | |
| | | | | | | | | |
| | | | | | | | | |
| | | | | | | | | |
| | | | | | | | | |
| | | | | | | | | |
| | | | | | | | | |
| | | | | | | | | |
| | | | | | | | | |
| | | | | | | | | |
| | | | | | | | | |
| | | | | | | | | |

Name _____

# Consonant Blends

Name each picture.
Fill in the circle next to the sounds you hear at the beginning of each word.

1. ○ st ○ sk ○ sl

2. ○ st ○ sk ○ sw

3. ○ st ○ sk ○ sw

4. ○ sp ○ sk ○ sw

5. ○ sp ○ sk ○ sw

6. ○ st ○ sk ○ sl

7. ○ sp ○ sk ○ sl

8. ○ st ○ sk ○ sw

# Distinguishes Between Consonant Blends: *bl, cl, fl, gl, pl, sl*

**Quick Checks**

## Objective:

Student distinguishes consonant blends *bl, cl, fl, gl, pl,* and *sl.*

## Materials:

Mat, p. 91

Word Cards, p. 93

Class Checklist, p. 95

Activity Sheet, p. 96

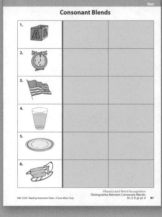

## Model the Task

Place the mat on the table. Place the word cards faceup in a row on the table. Say:

> Look at the pictures on the mat. Listen to the beginning sounds as I say each picture name.

Point to each picture as you name it. Say:

> Block, clock, flag, glass, plate, sled.
>
> Now look at the word cards. I will place a word card next to the picture with the same beginning sounds.

Place the *bleed* word card on the mat in the first box next to the block. Say:

> Bleed. *Bleed* begins with /bl/, so it belongs in the box next to the block. Bleed, block. Both words begin with /bl/.

## Student Task

> Now it's your turn. Pick up a card and read the word to me.

Student responds. Say:

> Now place it in one of the boxes on the mat next to the picture with the same beginning sounds.

Student responds. Record the student's response on the class checklist. Say:

> Now choose another card and read the word to me.

Student responds. Say:

> Place the card in one of the boxes on the mat next to the picture with the same beginning sounds.

Record the student's response on the class checklist. Repeat the procedure and the script modeled above for each of the remaining word cards.

# Consonant Blends

| | | |
|---|---|---|
| 1. | | |
| 2. | | |
| 3. | | |
| 4. | | |
| 5. | | |
| 6. | | |

**Phonics and Word Recognition**
Distinguishes Between Consonant Blends:
*bl, cl, fl, gl, pl, sl*

**Distinguishes Between Consonant Blends:**
*bl, cl, fl, gl, pl, sl*

Phonics and Word Recognition

EMC 3339 • © Evan-Moor Corp.

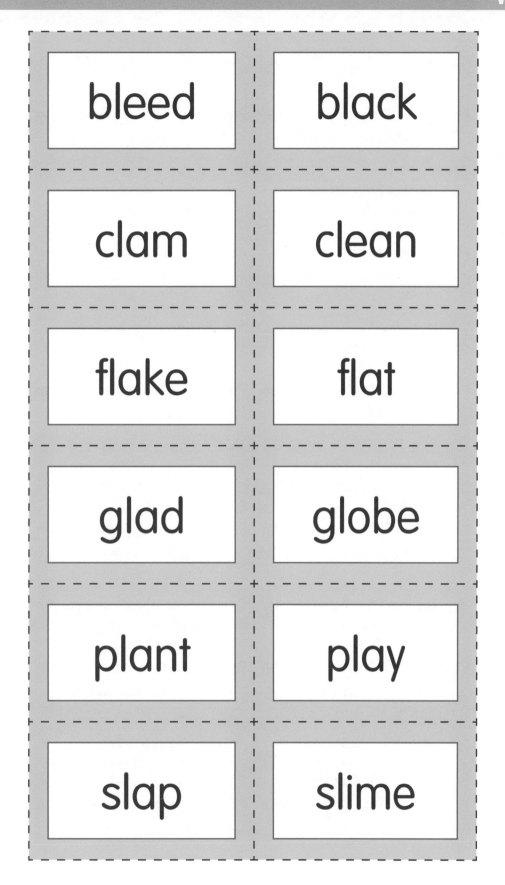

| bleed | black |
| clam | clean |
| flake | flat |
| glad | globe |
| plant | play |
| slap | slime |

**Phonics and Word Recognition**
Distinguishes Between Consonant Blends:
*bl, cl, fl, gl, pl, sl*    **93**

**Distinguishes Between
Consonant Blends:**
*bl, cl, fl, gl, pl, sl*

Phonics and Word Recognition

EMC 3339 • © Evan-Moor Corp.

**Distinguishes Between
Consonant Blends:**
*bl, cl, fl, gl, pl, sl*

Phonics and Word Recognition

EMC 3339 • © Evan-Moor Corp.

**Distinguishes Between
Consonant Blends:**
*bl, cl, fl, gl, pl, sl*

Phonics and Word Recognition

EMC 3339 • © Evan-Moor Corp.

**Distinguishes Between
Consonant Blends:**
*bl, cl, fl, gl, pl, sl*

Phonics and Word Recognition

EMC 3339 • © Evan-Moor Corp.

**Distinguishes Between
Consonant Blends:**
*bl, cl, fl, gl, pl, sl*

Phonics and Word Recognition

EMC 3339 • © Evan-Moor Corp.

**Distinguishes Between
Consonant Blends:**
*bl, cl, fl, gl, pl, sl*

Phonics and Word Recognition

EMC 3339 • © Evan-Moor Corp.

**Distinguishes Between
Consonant Blends:**
*bl, cl, fl, gl, pl, sl*

Phonics and Word Recognition

EMC 3339 • © Evan-Moor Corp.

**Distinguishes Between
Consonant Blends:**
*bl, cl, fl, gl, pl, sl*

Phonics and Word Recognition

EMC 3339 • © Evan-Moor Corp.

**Distinguishes Between
Consonant Blends:**
*bl, cl, fl, gl, pl, sl*

Phonics and Word Recognition

EMC 3339 • © Evan-Moor Corp.

**Distinguishes Between
Consonant Blends:**
*bl, cl, fl, gl, pl, sl*

Phonics and Word Recognition

EMC 3339 • © Evan-Moor Corp.

**Distinguishes Between
Consonant Blends:**
*bl, cl, fl, gl, pl, sl*

Phonics and Word Recognition

EMC 3339 • © Evan-Moor Corp.

**Distinguishes Between
Consonant Blends:**
*bl, cl, fl, gl, pl, sl*

Phonics and Word Recognition

EMC 3339 • © Evan-Moor Corp.

# Distinguishes Between Consonant Blends: *bl, cl, fl, gl, pl, sl*

| Class Checklist | | Key: | **+** correct response | **−** incorrect response | | **●** self-corrected | | |
|---|---|---|---|---|---|---|---|---|
| Name | Date | **bl:** bleed black | **cl:** clam clean | **fl:** flake flat | **gl:** glad globe | **pl:** plant play | **sl:** slap slime | Notes |
| | | | | | | | | |
| | | | | | | | | |
| | | | | | | | | |
| | | | | | | | | |
| | | | | | | | | |
| | | | | | | | | |
| | | | | | | | | |
| | | | | | | | | |
| | | | | | | | | |
| | | | | | | | | |
| | | | | | | | | |
| | | | | | | | | |
| | | | | | | | | |
| | | | | | | | | |
| | | | | | | | | |
| | | | | | | | | |
| | | | | | | | | |
| | | | | | | | | |
| | | | | | | | | |
| | | | | | | | | |
| | | | | | | | | |
| | | | | | | | | |

**Phonics and Word Recognition**
Distinguishes Between Consonant Blends:
*bl, cl, fl, gl, pl, sl*

Name _____

# Write the Word

Name each picture.
Fill in the circle next to the sounds you hear at the beginning of each word.

| | |
|---|---|
| 1. ⃝ bl  ⃝ gl  ⃝ fl | 2. ⃝ fl  ⃝ pl  ⃝ sl |
| 3. ⃝ cl  ⃝ bl  ⃝ gl | 4. ⃝ fl  ⃝ pl  ⃝ sl |
| 5. ⃝ fl  ⃝ pl  ⃝ sl | 6. ⃝ sl  ⃝ cl  ⃝ pl |
| 7. ⃝ gl  ⃝ bl  ⃝ sl | 8. ⃝ cl  ⃝ fl  ⃝ pl |

# Identifies and Reads Word Families

## Objective:
Student reads and sorts word family words.

## Materials:
Word Cards, p. 99

Class Checklist, p. 101

Activity Sheet, p. 102

## Student Task

Place word family cards 1–6 in a row on the table. Leave space below each card in order for the student to place multiple cards below it. Place the remaining word family cards faceup in a pile. Say:

> Today we are going to read words and put them with their word family. We have six word family groups. Let's begin.

> Pick a card from the pile. Read the word to me.

Student responds. Say:

> Place the card below the word family it belongs to.

Record the student's response on the class checklist. Say:

> Pick another card. Read the word to me.

Student responds. Say:

> Place the card below the word family it belongs to.

Student responds. Say:

> Keep picking cards and placing them below the word family they belong to.

Record the student's responses on the class checklist.

1.

| pain | rain | train |

2.

| care | dare | scare |

3.

| fair | chair | stair |

4.

| few | new | chew |

5.

| found | ground | sound |

6.

| book | cook | shook |

**Phonics and Word Recognition**
Identifies and Reads Word Families **99**

| Identifies and Reads Word Families | Identifies and Reads Word Families | Identifies and Reads Word Families |
|---|---|---|
| **Phonics and Word Recognition** | **Phonics and Word Recognition** | **Phonics and Word Recognition** |
| EMC 3339 • © Evan-Moor Corp. | EMC 3339 • © Evan-Moor Corp. | EMC 3339 • © Evan-Moor Corp. |
| **Identifies and Reads Word Families** | **Identifies and Reads Word Families** | **Identifies and Reads Word Families** |
| **Phonics and Word Recognition** | **Phonics and Word Recognition** | **Phonics and Word Recognition** |
| EMC 3339 • © Evan-Moor Corp. | EMC 3339 • © Evan-Moor Corp. | EMC 3339 • © Evan-Moor Corp. |
| **Identifies and Reads Word Families** | **Identifies and Reads Word Families** | **Identifies and Reads Word Families** |
| **Phonics and Word Recognition** | **Phonics and Word Recognition** | **Phonics and Word Recognition** |
| EMC 3339 • © Evan-Moor Corp. | EMC 3339 • © Evan-Moor Corp. | EMC 3339 • © Evan-Moor Corp. |
| **Identifies and Reads Word Families** | **Identifies and Reads Word Families** | **Identifies and Reads Word Families** |
| **Phonics and Word Recognition** | **Phonics and Word Recognition** | **Phonics and Word Recognition** |
| EMC 3339 • © Evan-Moor Corp. | EMC 3339 • © Evan-Moor Corp. | EMC 3339 • © Evan-Moor Corp. |
| **Identifies and Reads Word Families** | **Identifies and Reads Word Families** | **Identifies and Reads Word Families** |
| **Phonics and Word Recognition** | **Phonics and Word Recognition** | **Phonics and Word Recognition** |
| EMC 3339 • © Evan-Moor Corp. | EMC 3339 • © Evan-Moor Corp. | EMC 3339 • © Evan-Moor Corp. |
| **Identifies and Reads Word Families** | **Identifies and Reads Word Families** | **Identifies and Reads Word Families** |
| **Phonics and Word Recognition** | **Phonics and Word Recognition** | **Phonics and Word Recognition** |
| EMC 3339 • © Evan-Moor Corp. | EMC 3339 • © Evan-Moor Corp. | EMC 3339 • © Evan-Moor Corp. |

# Identifies and Reads Word Families

| Name | Date | -ain: pain rain train | -are: care dare scare | -air: fair chair stair | -ew: few new chew | -ound: found ground sound | -ook: book cook shook | Notes |
|------|------|------|------|------|------|------|------|-------|
| | | | | | | | | |
| | | | | | | | | |
| | | | | | | | | |
| | | | | | | | | |
| | | | | | | | | |
| | | | | | | | | |
| | | | | | | | | |
| | | | | | | | | |
| | | | | | | | | |
| | | | | | | | | |
| | | | | | | | | |
| | | | | | | | | |
| | | | | | | | | |
| | | | | | | | | |
| | | | | | | | | |
| | | | | | | | | |
| | | | | | | | | |
| | | | | | | | | |
| | | | | | | | | |
| | | | | | | | | |
| | | | | | | | | |
| | | | | | | | | |

**Class Checklist**

**Key:** **+** correct response   **–** incorrect response   **•** self-corrected

Note: Student writes a letter on each line to complete the word family.

Name _____

# Word Family Words

Write a letter on each line to complete the word family.

**train**

____ ain

____ ain

r    p

**chair**

____ air

____ ____ air

f    st

**book**

____ ook

____ ook

c    t

**sound**

____ ound

____ ound

f    p

**stew**

____ ____ ew

____ ____ ew

kn    bl

**scare**

____ are

____ are

d    c

### Unit 3
# Vocabulary and Concept Development

# Reads and Understands Antonyms

**Objective:**
Student reads and matches antonyms.

**Materials:**
Mat, p. 107
Word Cards, p. 109
Class Checklist, p. 111
Activity Sheet, p. 112

## Student Task

Place the mat on the table. Place the word cards faceup in a row on the table. Say:

> Today we are going to match words that are antonyms. Antonyms are word pairs that mean opposite things. Let's begin.

Point to the first word on the mat. Say:

> Read the first word on the mat to me.

Student responds. Say:

> Look at the word cards and find the antonym for *clean*. Place the card next to *clean* on the mat.

Student responds. Say:

> Read the next word to me.

Student responds. Say:

> Find the antonym for *small* and place it on the mat.

Student responds.

Repeat the procedure and the script modeled above for each of the words on the mat.

Use the mat as a reference to record the student's responses on the class checklist.

# Antonyms

| | |
|---|---|
| clean | |
| small | |
| push | |
| night | |
| quiet | |
| float | |
| start | |
| under | |

Vocabulary and Concept Development
Reads and Understands Antonyms **107**

**Reads and Understands Antonyms**

Vocabulary and Concept Development

EMC 3339 • © Evan-Moor Corp.

| | |
|---|---|
| dirty | large |
| pull | day |
| noisy | sink |
| finish | over |

**Vocabulary and Concept Development**
Reads and Understands Antonyms    **109**

**Reads and Understands Antonyms**

Vocabulary and Concept Development

EMC 3339 • © Evan-Moor Corp.

**Reads and Understands Antonyms**

Vocabulary and Concept Development

EMC 3339 • © Evan-Moor Corp.

**Reads and Understands Antonyms**

Vocabulary and Concept Development

EMC 3339 • © Evan-Moor Corp.

**Reads and Understands Antonyms**

Vocabulary and Concept Development

EMC 3339 • © Evan-Moor Corp.

**Reads and Understands Antonyms**

Vocabulary and Concept Development

EMC 3339 • © Evan-Moor Corp.

**Reads and Understands Antonyms**

Vocabulary and Concept Development

EMC 3339 • © Evan-Moor Corp.

**Reads and Understands Antonyms**

Vocabulary and Concept Development

EMC 3339 • © Evan-Moor Corp.

**Reads and Understands Antonyms**

Vocabulary and Concept Development

EMC 3339 • © Evan-Moor Corp.

# Reads and Understands Antonyms

| Class Checklist | | Key:  **+** correct response    **–** incorrect response    ● self-corrected | | | | | | | | |
|---|---|---|---|---|---|---|---|---|---|---|
| Name | Date | clean/ dirty | small/ large | push/ pull | night/ day | quiet/ noisy | float/ sink | start/ finish | under/ over | Notes |
| | | | | | | | | | | |
| | | | | | | | | | | |
| | | | | | | | | | | |
| | | | | | | | | | | |
| | | | | | | | | | | |
| | | | | | | | | | | |
| | | | | | | | | | | |
| | | | | | | | | | | |
| | | | | | | | | | | |
| | | | | | | | | | | |
| | | | | | | | | | | |
| | | | | | | | | | | |
| | | | | | | | | | | |
| | | | | | | | | | | |
| | | | | | | | | | | |
| | | | | | | | | | | |
| | | | | | | | | | | |
| | | | | | | | | | | |
| | | | | | | | | | | |
| | | | | | | | | | | |
| | | | | | | | | | | |
| | | | | | | | | | | |

Name _____

# Antonyms

Read each sentence. Look at the bold word.
Fill in the circle next to the word that means the opposite.

open

| | |
|---|---|
| **1.** <br><br> I am **sad**. <br><br> ○ small   ○ happy   ○ unhappy | **2.** <br><br> I went **up** the stairs. <br><br> ○ down   ○ beside   ○ above |
| **3.** <br><br> The ground is **dry**. <br><br> ○ clean   ○ hot   ○ wet | **4.** <br><br> The store was **open**. <br><br> ○ finished   ○ closed   ○ big |
| **5.** <br><br> He will **stop** the motor. <br><br> ○ go   ○ end   ○ start | **6.** <br><br> The baby is sleeping. <br> Please be **quiet**. <br><br> ○ little   ○ noisy   ○ wet |
| **7.** <br><br> My friend is **mean**. <br><br> ○ nice   ○ angry   ○ sad | **8.** <br><br> My shoes are **old**. <br><br> ○ used   ○ new   ○ fast |

closed

# Reads and Understands Synonyms

## Objective:

Student reads and matches synonyms.

## Materials:

Mat, p. 115

Word Cards, p. 117

Class Checklist, p. 119

Activity Sheet, p. 120

## Student Task

Place the mat on the table. Place the word cards faceup in a row on the table. Say:

> Today we are going to match words that are synonyms. Synonyms are word pairs that mean the same thing. Let's begin.

Point to the first word on the mat. Say:

> Read the first word on the mat to me.

Student responds. Say:

> Look at the word cards and find the synonym for *part*. Place the card next to *part* on the mat.

Student responds. Say:

> Read the next word to me.

Student responds. Say:

> Find the synonym for *large* and place it on the mat.

Student responds.

Repeat the procedure and the script modeled above for each of the words on the mat.

Use the mat as a reference to record the student's responses on the class checklist.

# Synonyms

| | |
|---|---|
| part | |
| large | |
| quick | |
| build | |
| friend | |
| trash | |
| celebration | |
| yell | |

Vocabulary and Concept Development
Reads and Understands Synonyms **115**

**Reads and Understands Synonyms**

| | |
|---|---|
| piece | pal |
| huge | garbage |
| fast | party |
| make | shout |

Vocabulary and Concept Development
Reads and Understands Synonyms    **117**

**Reads and Understands Synonyms**

Vocabulary and Concept Development

EMC 3339 • © Evan-Moor Corp.

**Reads and Understands Synonyms**

Vocabulary and Concept Development

EMC 3339 • © Evan-Moor Corp.

**Reads and Understands Synonyms**

Vocabulary and Concept Development

EMC 3339 • © Evan-Moor Corp.

**Reads and Understands Synonyms**

Vocabulary and Concept Development

EMC 3339 • © Evan-Moor Corp.

**Reads and Understands Synonyms**

Vocabulary and Concept Development

EMC 3339 • © Evan-Moor Corp.

**Reads and Understands Synonyms**

Vocabulary and Concept Development

EMC 3339 • © Evan-Moor Corp.

**Reads and Understands Synonyms**

Vocabulary and Concept Development

EMC 3339 • © Evan-Moor Corp.

**Reads and Understands Synonyms**

Vocabulary and Concept Development

EMC 3339 • © Evan-Moor Corp.

# Reads and Understands Synonyms

| Class Checklist | | Key: + correct response — incorrect response • self-corrected | | | | | | | | |
|---|---|---|---|---|---|---|---|---|---|---|
| Name | Date | part/ piece | large/ huge | quick/ fast | build/ make | friend/ pal | trash/ garbage | celebra- tion/ party | yell/ shout | Notes |
| | | | | | | | | | | |
| | | | | | | | | | | |
| | | | | | | | | | | |
| | | | | | | | | | | |
| | | | | | | | | | | |
| | | | | | | | | | | |
| | | | | | | | | | | |
| | | | | | | | | | | |
| | | | | | | | | | | |
| | | | | | | | | | | |
| | | | | | | | | | | |
| | | | | | | | | | | |
| | | | | | | | | | | |
| | | | | | | | | | | |
| | | | | | | | | | | |
| | | | | | | | | | | |
| | | | | | | | | | | |
| | | | | | | | | | | |
| | | | | | | | | | | |
| | | | | | | | | | | |
| | | | | | | | | | | |
| | | | | | | | | | | |
| | | | | | | | | | | |

Note: Student identifies synonyms.

Name _____

# The Same

Read each sentence.
Look at the bold word.
Fill in the circle next to the word that means the same.

| | |
|---|---|
| **1.**<br><br>I will **close** the door.<br><br>○ shut ○ open ○ hammer | **2.**<br><br>I am ready to **go**.<br><br>○ stay ○ leave ○ play |
| **3.**<br><br>I **start** school today.<br><br>○ stop ○ leave ○ begin | **4.**<br><br>You don't need to **shout**.<br><br>○ yell ○ cry ○ play |
| **5.**<br><br>Spot is a **large** dog.<br><br>○ small ○ big ○ old | **6.**<br><br>Put it in the **trash**.<br><br>○ car ○ room ○ garbage |
| **7.**<br><br>A cat runs **fast**.<br><br>○ quickly ○ slow ○ new | **8.**<br><br>May I have a **piece** of it?<br><br>○ none ○ part ○ whole |

# Matches Words with Prefixes

## Objective:
Student matches words with the correct prefix and then reads the words.

## Materials:
Mat, p. 123

Word Cards, p. 125

Class Checklist, p. 127

Activity Sheet, p. 128

# Model the Task

Place the mat on the table. Place the word cards in a pile on the table. Place *true* at the top of the pile. Say:

> Today we are going to match each word with the correct prefix.

Choose the *true* word card. Say:

> True.

Place the *true* word card next to *re* on the mat. Say:

> Retrue. *Retrue* is not a word.

Place the *true* word card next to *un* on the mat. Say:

> Untrue. The correct prefix is *un*. *Untrue* is a word.

# Student Task

> Now it's your turn. Choose a card and read the word to me.

Student responds. Say:

> Now place the card next to the correct prefix on the mat. Then read the new word to me.

Student responds. Record the student's response on the class checklist. Remove the word card from the mat. Say:

> Choose another card and read the word to me.

Student responds. Say:

> Place the card next to the correct prefix on the mat. Read the new word to me.

Student responds. Record the student's response on the class checklist. Clear the mat. Repeat the procedure and the script modeled above for each of the remaining word cards.

# Prefixes

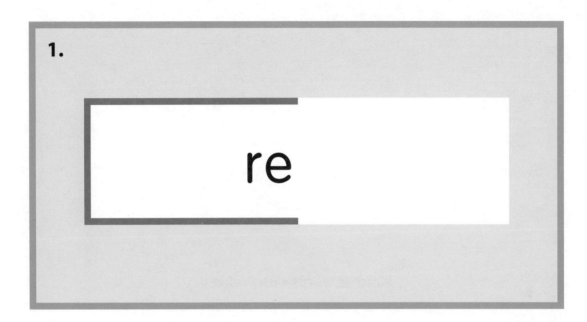

Vocabulary and Concept Development
Matches Words with Prefixes  **123**

## Matches Words with Prefixes

EMC 3339 • © Evan-Moor Corp.

true

copy

turn

cycle

able

write

Vocabulary and Concept Development
Matches Words with Prefixes  **125**

**Matches Words with Prefixes**

Vocabulary and Concept
Development

EMC 3339 • © Evan-Moor Corp.

**Matches Words with Prefixes**

Vocabulary and Concept
Development

EMC 3339 • © Evan-Moor Corp.

**Matches Words with Prefixes**

Vocabulary and Concept
Development

EMC 3339 • © Evan-Moor Corp.

**Matches Words with Prefixes**

Vocabulary and Concept
Development

EMC 3339 • © Evan-Moor Corp.

**Matches Words with Prefixes**

Vocabulary and Concept
Development

EMC 3339 • © Evan-Moor Corp.

**Matches Words with Prefixes**

Vocabulary and Concept
Development

EMC 3339 • © Evan-Moor Corp.

# Matches Words with Prefixes

| Class Checklist | | Key: + correct response  − incorrect response  • self-corrected | | | | | | |
|---|---|---|---|---|---|---|---|---|
| Name | Date | recopy | recycle | rewrite | return | untrue | unable | Notes |
| | | | | | | | | |
| | | | | | | | | |
| | | | | | | | | |
| | | | | | | | | |
| | | | | | | | | |
| | | | | | | | | |
| | | | | | | | | |
| | | | | | | | | |
| | | | | | | | | |
| | | | | | | | | |
| | | | | | | | | |
| | | | | | | | | |
| | | | | | | | | |
| | | | | | | | | |
| | | | | | | | | |
| | | | | | | | | |
| | | | | | | | | |
| | | | | | | | | |
| | | | | | | | | |
| | | | | | | | | |
| | | | | | | | | |
| | | | | | | | | |
| | | | | | | | | |
| | | | | | | | | |

Vocabulary and Concept Development

**Activity Sheet**

Name _____

# *un* or *re*?

Fill in the circle next to the correct prefix for each word.
Then write the prefix **un** or **re** to make a word.

| | | |
|---|---|---|
| 1. _____real<br><br>○ un   ○ re | 2. _____heat<br><br>○ un   ○ re | 3. _____pay<br><br>○ un   ○ re |
| 4. _____paint<br><br>○ un   ○ re | 5. _____buckle<br><br>○ un   ○ re | 6. _____build<br><br>○ un   ○ re |
| 7. _____fair<br><br>○ un   ○ re | 8. _____read<br><br>○ un   ○ re | 9. _____selfish<br><br>○ un   ○ re |

# Matches Words with Suffixes

## Objective:

Student matches words with the correct suffix and then reads the words.

## Materials:

Mat, p. 131

Word Cards, p. 133

Class Checklist, p. 135

Activity Sheet, p. 136

## Model the Task

Place the mat on the table. Place the word cards in a pile on the table. Place *care* at the top of the pile. Say:

> Today we are going to match each word with the correct suffix.

Choose the *care* word card. Say:

> Care.

Place the *care* word card next to *ful* on the mat. Say:

> Careful. *Careful* is a word. The correct suffix is *ful.*

## Student Task

> Now it's your turn. Choose a card and read the word to me.

Student responds. Say:

> Now place the card next to the correct suffix on the mat. Then read the new word to me.

Student responds. Record the student's response on the class checklist. Remove the word card from the mat. Say:

> Choose another card and read the word to me.

Student responds. Say:

> Place the card next to the correct suffix on the mat. Read the new word to me.

Student responds. Record the student's response on the class checklist. Clear the mat. Repeat the procedure and the script modeled above for each of the remaining word cards.

# Suffixes

### 1.

### 2.

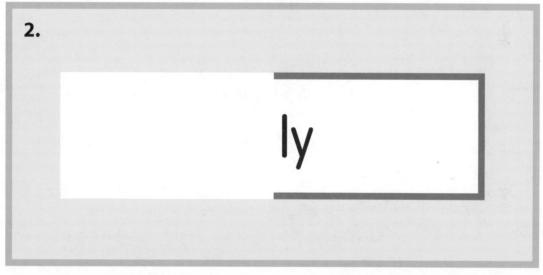

### 3.

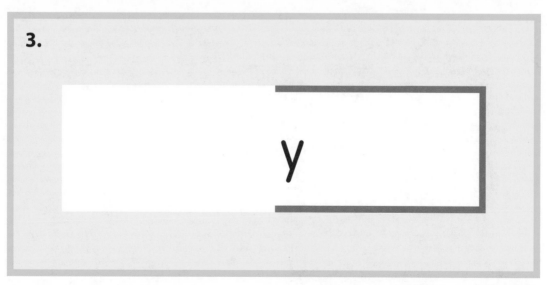

**Matches Words with Suffixes**

Vocabulary and Concept Development

EMC 3339 • © Evan-Moor Corp.

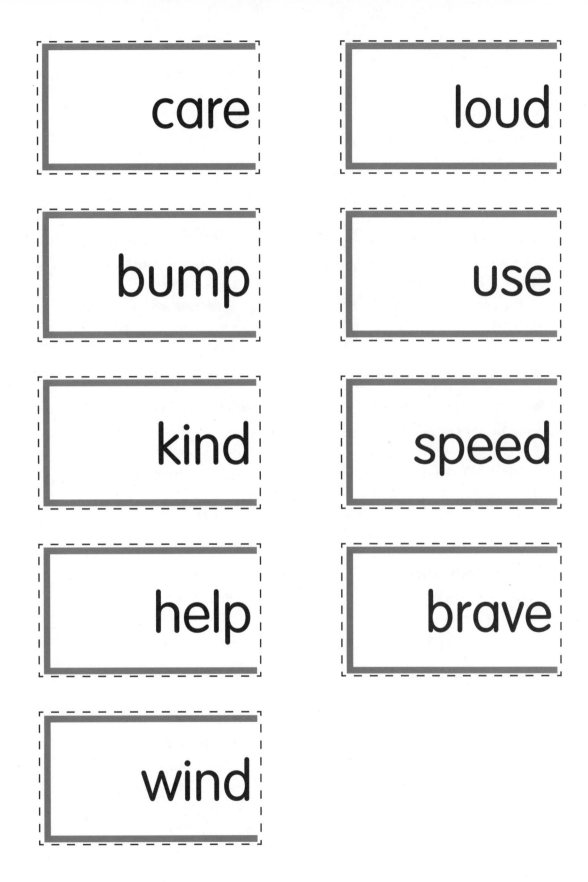

care

loud

bump

use

kind

speed

help

brave

wind

Vocabulary and Concept Development
Matches Words with Suffixes    **133**

**Matches Words with Suffixes**

Vocabulary and Concept
Development

EMC 3339 • © Evan-Moor Corp.

**Matches Words with Suffixes**

Vocabulary and Concept
Development

EMC 3339 • © Evan-Moor Corp.

**Matches Words with Suffixes**

Vocabulary and Concept
Development

EMC 3339 • © Evan-Moor Corp.

**Matches Words with Suffixes**

Vocabulary and Concept
Development

EMC 3339 • © Evan-Moor Corp.

**Matches Words with Suffixes**

Vocabulary and Concept
Development

EMC 3339 • © Evan-Moor Corp.

**Matches Words with Suffixes**

Vocabulary and Concept
Development

EMC 3339 • © Evan-Moor Corp.

**Matches Words with Suffixes**

Vocabulary and Concept
Development

EMC 3339 • © Evan-Moor Corp.

**Matches Words with Suffixes**

Vocabulary and Concept
Development

EMC 3339 • © Evan-Moor Corp.

**Matches Words with Suffixes**

Vocabulary and Concept
Development

EMC 3339 • © Evan-Moor Corp.

# Matches Words with Suffixes

| Class Checklist | | Key: + correct response  − incorrect response  • self-corrected | | | | | | | | | | |
|---|---|---|---|---|---|---|---|---|---|---|---|---|
| Name | Date | careful | useful | helpful | loudly | kindly | bravely | bumpy | speedy | windy | Notes |
| | | | | | | | | | | | |
| | | | | | | | | | | | |
| | | | | | | | | | | | |
| | | | | | | | | | | | |
| | | | | | | | | | | | |
| | | | | | | | | | | | |
| | | | | | | | | | | | |
| | | | | | | | | | | | |
| | | | | | | | | | | | |
| | | | | | | | | | | | |
| | | | | | | | | | | | |
| | | | | | | | | | | | |
| | | | | | | | | | | | |
| | | | | | | | | | | | |
| | | | | | | | | | | | |
| | | | | | | | | | | | |
| | | | | | | | | | | | |
| | | | | | | | | | | | |
| | | | | | | | | | | | |
| | | | | | | | | | | | |
| | | | | | | | | | | | |
| | | | | | | | | | | | |

Name _____

# The End

Fill in the circle next to the correct suffix.
Then write the suffix on the line to make a word.

| | | |
|---|---|---|
| **1.**<br><br>color_____<br><br>○ ful<br>○ ly<br>○ y | **2.**<br><br>nice_____<br><br>○ ful<br>○ ly<br>○ y | **3.**<br><br>chill_____<br><br>○ ful<br>○ ly<br>○ y |
| **4.**<br><br>rain_____<br><br>○ ful<br>○ ly<br>○ y | **5.**<br><br>safe_____<br><br>○ ful<br>○ ly<br>○ y | **6.**<br><br>play_____<br><br>○ ful<br>○ ly<br>○ y |
| **7.**<br><br>dirt_____<br><br>○ ful<br>○ ly<br>○ y | **8.**<br><br>use_____<br><br>○ ful<br>○ ly<br>○ y | **9.**<br><br>slow_____<br><br>○ ful<br>○ ly<br>○ y |

# Uses Multiple-Meaning Words

## Objective:

Student chooses the correct multiple-meaning word and places it next to the corresponding definitions. Then the student uses the word in a sentence.

## Materials:

Mat, p. 139

Word Cards, p. 141

Class Checklist, p. 143

Activity Sheet, p. 144

## Student Task

Place the mat on the table. Place the word cards faceup in a row. Say:

> Today we are going to work with words that have more than one meaning. Let's begin.

> Look at the mat. The first definition says, "a stone." The second says, "to move back and forth."

> Which card shows a word that means both of these things?

Student responds. Say:

> Read the word to me and place the card next to the definitions on the mat.

Student responds. Say:

> Now use the word *rock* in a sentence that uses the meaning "a stone."

Student responds. Repeat the procedure and the script modeled above for each of the four remaining multiple-meaning words. See below for sentence requests.

### Sentence Requests

**Plant:** Use the word *plant* in a sentence that uses the meaning *a growing thing*.

**Bark:** Use the word *bark* in a sentence that uses the meaning *the sound a dog makes*.

**Right:** Use the word *right* in a sentence that uses the meaning *a direction*.

**Check:** Use the word *check* in a sentence that uses the meaning *to look over*.

# Multiple-Meaning Words

| | |
|---|---|
| | 1. a stone |
| | 2. to move back and forth |
| | 1. a growing thing |
| | 2. to put seeds in the ground |
| | 1. the sound a dog makes |
| | 2. the outside covering of a tree |
| | 1. a direction |
| | 2. being correct |
| | 1. to look over |
| | 2. a piece of paper you write on and use in place of money |

**Uses Multiple-Meaning Words**

Vocabulary and Concept Development

EMC 3339 • © Evan-Moor Corp.

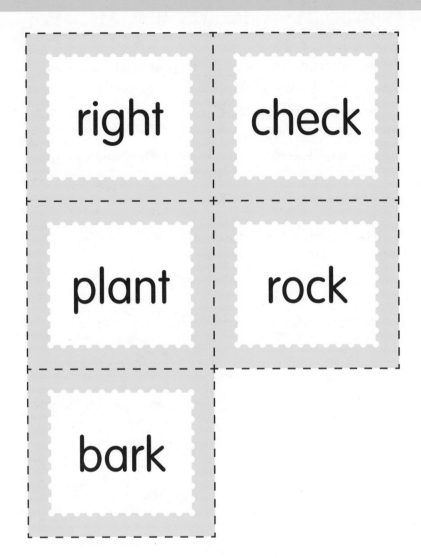

**Uses Multiple-Meaning Words**

Vocabulary and Concept Development

EMC 3339 • © Evan-Moor Corp.

**Uses Multiple-Meaning Words**

Vocabulary and Concept Development

EMC 3339 • © Evan-Moor Corp.

**Uses Multiple-Meaning Words**

Vocabulary and Concept Development

EMC 3339 • © Evan-Moor Corp.

**Uses Multiple-Meaning Words**

Vocabulary and Concept Development

EMC 3339 • © Evan-Moor Corp.

**Uses Multiple-Meaning Words**

Vocabulary and Concept Development

EMC 3339 • © Evan-Moor Corp.

# Uses Multiple-Meaning Words

| Class Checklist | | Key: + correct response    − incorrect response    ● self-corrected | | | | | |
|---|---|---|---|---|---|---|---|
| Name | Date | rock | plant | bark | right | check | Notes |
| | | | | | | | |
| | | | | | | | |
| | | | | | | | |
| | | | | | | | |
| | | | | | | | |
| | | | | | | | |
| | | | | | | | |
| | | | | | | | |
| | | | | | | | |
| | | | | | | | |
| | | | | | | | |
| | | | | | | | |
| | | | | | | | |
| | | | | | | | |
| | | | | | | | |
| | | | | | | | |
| | | | | | | | |
| | | | | | | | |
| | | | | | | | |
| | | | | | | | |
| | | | | | | | |
| | | | | | | | |
| | | | | | | | |

Name _____

# Multiple-Meaning Words

Read each sentence. Look at the bold word.
Fill in the circle next to the correct definition of the word.

---

**1.**

I ate a **roll** with my soup.

○ to turn over and over

○ a kind of bread

**2.**

I threw a **rock**.

○ a stone

○ to move back and forth

---

**3.**

I have **pet** hamster.

○ to stroke or pat

○ a tame animal that lives
with a person

**4.**

You need a **stamp** to mail
a letter.

○ small sticker used on mail

○ to put a foot down loudly

---

**5.**

Blue is my favorite **color**.

○ to use a crayon on paper

○ red, yellow, orange, green

**6.**

I use sticks to build a **fire**.

○ intense heat

○ to ask a person to leave
a job

---

## Unit 4
# Reading Comprehension

EMC 3339 • Reading Assessment Tasks • © Evan-Moor Corp.

**Objective:**
Student shows an understanding of cause-and-effect relationships.

**Materials:**
Mat, p. 149

Cards, p. 151

Class Checklist, p. 153

Activity Sheet, p. 154

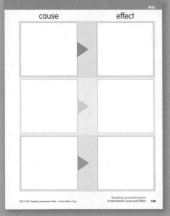

## Student Task

Place the mat on the table. Place the cards faceup in a row on the table. Say:

> Look at these pictures. Some pictures show *why* something happened and some pictures show *what* happened. We call this the *cause* and the *effect*.

> You will find the picture pairs that belong together and decide which picture shows the cause and which picture shows the effect. Let's begin.

Point to the *cause* and *effect* boxes on the mat. Say:

> Look at each picture and read the sentences. Place the picture that shows *what* happened under *effect*. Place the picture that shows *why* it happened under *cause*.

> Place all the picture pairs on the mat.

Student responds. Use the mat as a reference to record the student's responses on the class checklist.

# cause

# effect

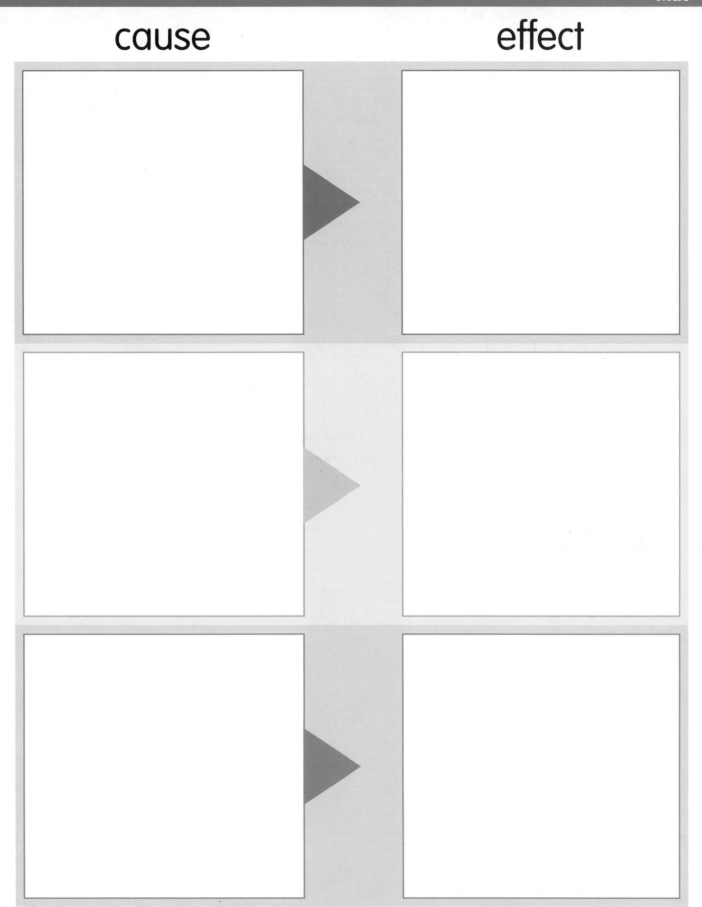

## Understands Cause and Effect

**Reading Comprehension**

EMC 3339 • © Evan-Moor Corp.

Pam ate six cookies and three bags of chips. Then she drank a can of soda.

Pam's stomach was full. Pam felt sick.

Ron was walking fast. He was not looking down.

Ron slipped on a banana peel and fell to the ground.

There were too many groceries in one bag. The bag was too full. The eggs were at the top.

The eggs fell to the floor and broke.

**Reading Comprehension**
Understands Cause and Effect    **151**

**Understands Cause and Effect**

**Reading Comprehension**

EMC 3339 • © Evan-Moor Corp.

**Understands Cause and Effect**

**Reading Comprehension**

EMC 3339 • © Evan-Moor Corp.

**Understands Cause and Effect**

**Reading Comprehension**

EMC 3339 • © Evan-Moor Corp.

**Understands Cause and Effect**

**Reading Comprehension**

EMC 3339 • © Evan-Moor Corp.

**Understands Cause and Effect**

**Reading Comprehension**

EMC 3339 • © Evan-Moor Corp.

**Understands Cause and Effect**

**Reading Comprehension**

EMC 3339 • © Evan-Moor Corp.

# Understands Cause and Effect

| Class Checklist | | Key:   + correct response    – incorrect response    • self-corrected | | |
|---|---|---|---|---|
| Name | Date | Eggs at Top of Grocery Bag/ Broken Eggs | Boy Stepping on Banana Peel/Boy Slipping on Banana Peel | Girl Eating Snacks/ Girl with Tummy Ache |
| | | | | |
| | | | | |
| | | | | |
| | | | | |
| | | | | |
| | | | | |
| | | | | |
| | | | | |
| | | | | |
| | | | | |
| | | | | |
| | | | | |
| | | | | |
| | | | | |
| | | | | |
| | | | | |
| | | | | |
| | | | | |
| | | | | |
| | | | | |
| | | | | |
| | | | | |
| | | | | |
| | | | | |

Note: Student shows an understanding of cause and effect.

Name _____

# Cause and Effect

Each picture shows the cause. Write about what you think the effect might be.

_____

_____

_____

_____

_____

_____

_____

_____

_____

## Objective:

Student follows written multiple-step directions using manipulatives.

## Materials:

Mat, p. 157

Direction Cards, p. 159

Picture Pieces, p. 161

Class Checklist, p. 163

Activity Sheet, p. 164

## Student Task

Place the mat on the table. Place the picture pieces faceup in a row. Say:

> Today you are going to read directions and use the picture pieces and the mat to do what the directions ask. Let's begin.

> Read the directions on card 1. Follow the directions.

Student reads the directions and follows them. Record the student's response on the class checklist. Say:

> Read the directions on card 2. Follow the directions.

Student reads the directions and follows them. Record the student's response on the class checklist. Say:

> Now read the directions on card 3. Follow the directions.

Student reads the directions and follows them. Record the student's responses on the class checklist.

**1.**

Place one green apple and one red apple in the tree, and place one red apple on the ground below the tree.

**2.**

Place the boy on the bench and place the girl next to the flowers.

**3.**

Place the dog next to the tree, place the cat on the bench, and place one bird in the nest.

**Follows Written Multiple-Step Directions**

Reading Comprehension

EMC 3339 • © Evan-Moor Corp.

**Follows Written Multiple-Step Directions**

Reading Comprehension

EMC 3339 • © Evan-Moor Corp.

**Follows Written Multiple-Step Directions**

Reading Comprehension

EMC 3339 • © Evan-Moor Corp.

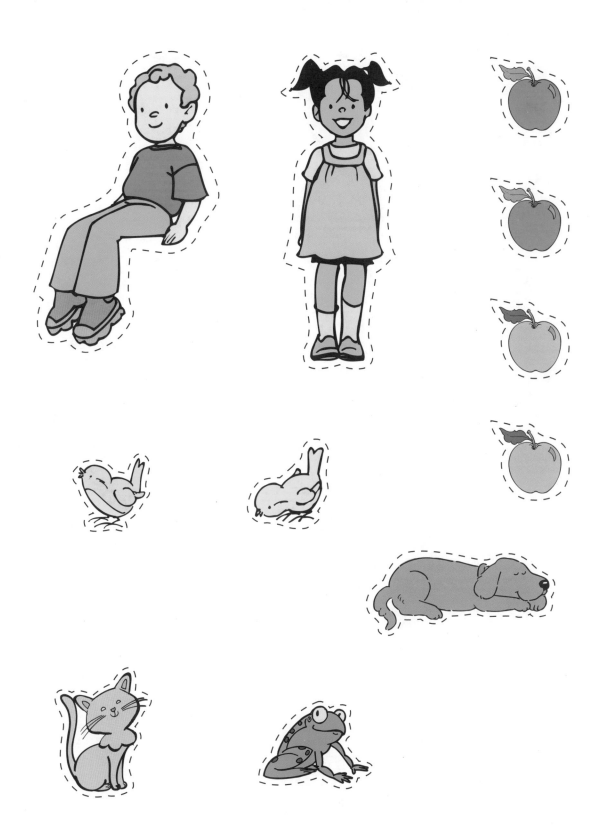

**Reading Comprehension**
Follows Written Multiple-Step Directions **161**

Follows Written
Multiple-Step
Directions
Reading
Comprehension
EMC 3339
© Evan-Moor Corp.

Follows Written
Multiple-Step
Directions
Reading
Comprehension
EMC 3339
© Evan-Moor Corp.

Follows Written
Multiple-Step
Directions
Reading
Comprehension
EMC 3339
© Evan-Moor Corp.

Follows Written
Multiple-Step
Directions
Reading
Comprehension
EMC 3339
© Evan-Moor Corp.

Follows Written
Multiple-Step
Directions
Reading
Comprehension
EMC 3339
© Evan-Moor Corp.

Follows Written
Multiple-Step
Directions
Reading
Comprehension
EMC 3339
© Evan-Moor Corp.

Follows Written
Multiple-Step Directions
Reading Comprehension
EMC 3339
© Evan-Moor Corp.

Follows Written
Multiple-Step Directions
Reading
Comprehension
EMC 3339
© Evan-Moor Corp.

Follows Written Multiple-Step Directions
Reading Comprehension
EMC 3339 • © Evan-Moor Corp.

Follows Written
Multiple-Step
Directions
Reading
Comprehension
EMC 3339
© Evan-Moor Corp.

Follows Written
Multiple-Step
Directions
Reading
Comprehension
EMC 3339
© Evan-Moor Corp.

# Follows Written Multiple-Step Directions

| Class Checklist | | Key: + correct response — incorrect response ● self-corrected | | | |
|---|---|---|---|---|---|
| Name | Date | **Card 1:** Green Apple in Tree Red Apple in Tree Red Apple on Ground | **Card 2:** Boy on Bench Girl next to Flowers | **Card 3:** Dog next to Tree Cat on Bench Bird in Nest | Notes |
| | | | | | |
| | | | | | |
| | | | | | |
| | | | | | |
| | | | | | |
| | | | | | |
| | | | | | |
| | | | | | |
| | | | | | |
| | | | | | |
| | | | | | |
| | | | | | |
| | | | | | |
| | | | | | |
| | | | | | |
| | | | | | |
| | | | | | |
| | | | | | |
| | | | | | |
| | | | | | |
| | | | | | |
| | | | | | |
| | | | | | |

Name _____

# Count the Overalls

Color the 2nd pair of overalls green.

Color the 5th pair of overalls orange.

Color the 3rd pair of overalls blue.

Color the 1st pair of overalls purple.

Color the 4th pair of overalls red.

**Objective:**

Student sequences sentences into a story.

**Materials:**

Mat, p. 167

Sentence Cards, p. 169

Class Checklist, p. 171

Activity Sheet, p. 172

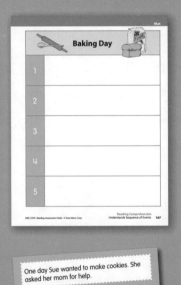

## Student Task

Place the mat on the table. Shuffle the sentence cards and place them faceup in a row on the table. Say:

> Today you are going to read sentences that tell a story. You decide which sentence should be first, second, third, fourth, and last. Let's begin.
>
> Read each of the cards. Then place them in order on the mat.

Student responds.

Once the student has finished placing all the cards on the mat, ask the student to read the story to you.

Record the student's responses on the class checklist.

# Baking Day

| | |
|---|---|
| **1** | |
| **2** | |
| **3** | |
| **4** | |
| **5** | |

**Reading Comprehension**
Understands Sequence of Events    **167**

**Understands Sequence of Events**

Reading Comprehension

EMC 3339 • © Evan-Moor Corp.

One day Sue wanted to make cookies. She asked her mom for help.

First, they mixed the flour, sugar, and baking soda.

Next, Sue added the butter and eggs while Mother poured in the chocolate chips.

Then, they put the dough on the cookie sheet. The cookies baked until they were done.

Finally, it was time for Sue and her mother to enjoy the freshly baked cookies.

**Understands Sequence of Events**

Reading Comprehension

EMC 3339 • © Evan-Moor Corp.


**Understands Sequence of Events**

Reading Comprehension

EMC 3339 • © Evan-Moor Corp.


**Understands Sequence of Events**

Reading Comprehension

EMC 3339 • © Evan-Moor Corp.


**Understands Sequence of Events**

Reading Comprehension

EMC 3339 • © Evan-Moor Corp.


**Understands Sequence of Events**

Reading Comprehension

EMC 3339 • © Evan-Moor Corp.

# Understands Sequence of Events

| Class Checklist | | | | |
|---|---|---|---|---|
| Name | Date | Correctly Sequenced the Sentences into a Story | Did Not Correctly Sequence the Sentences into a Story | Notes |
| | | | | |
| | | | | |
| | | | | |
| | | | | |
| | | | | |
| | | | | |
| | | | | |
| | | | | |
| | | | | |
| | | | | |
| | | | | |
| | | | | |
| | | | | |
| | | | | |
| | | | | |
| | | | | |
| | | | | |
| | | | | |
| | | | | |
| | | | | |
| | | | | |
| | | | | |
| | | | | |

Note: Student cuts and glues the pictures into sequential order.
Then the student writes a sentence next to each picture to tell a story.

Name _____

# Time for Bed

Look at each picture. Cut out the pictures and glue them in order.
Write a sentence next to each picture to tell a story.

| glue |
| :---: |
| glue |
| glue |
| glue |

1.

_____

2.

_____

3.

_____

4.

_____

**Reading Comprehension**

# Answer Key

## Page 12

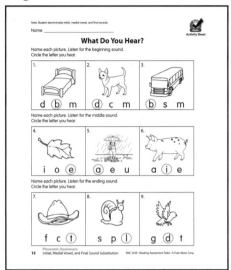

## Page 16

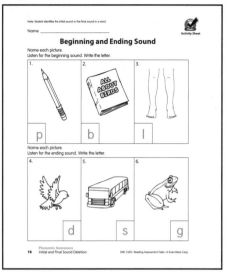

## Page 20

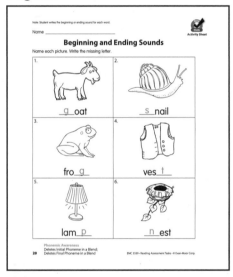

## Page 28

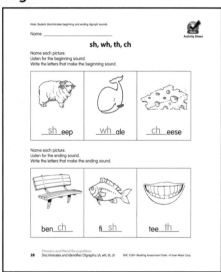

## Page 36

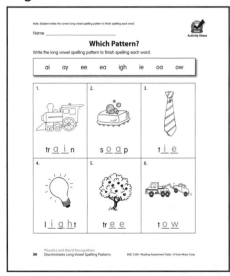

## Page 44

## Page 52

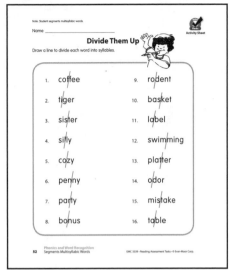

Note: Student segments multisyllabic words.

Name _____

### Divide Them Up

Draw a line to divide each word into syllables.

1. cof|fee
2. ti|ger
3. sis|ter
4. sil|ly
5. co|zy
6. pen|ny
7. par|ty
8. bo|nus
9. ro|dent
10. bas|ket
11. la|bel
12. swim|ming
13. plat|ter
14. o|dor
15. mis|take
16. ta|ble

Phonics and Word Recognition
52 Segments Multisyllabic Words                EMC 3339 • Reading Assessment Tasks • © Evan-Moor Corp.

## Page 58

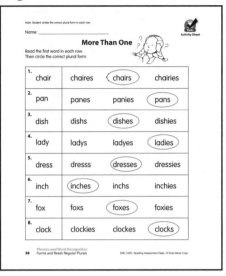

Note: Student circles the correct plural form in each row.

Name _____

### More Than One

Read the first word in each row.
Then circle the correct plural form.

| 1. chair | chaires | (chairs) | chairies |
| 2. pan | panes | panies | (pans) |
| 3. dish | dishs | (dishes) | dishies |
| 4. lady | ladys | ladyes | (ladies) |
| 5. dress | dresss | (dresses) | dressies |
| 6. inch | (inches) | inchs | inchies |
| 7. fox | foxs | (foxes) | foxies |
| 8. clock | clockies | clockes | (clocks) |

Phonics and Word Recognition
58 Forms and Reads Regular Plurals            EMC 3339 • Reading Assessment Tasks • © Evan-Moor Corp.

## Page 66

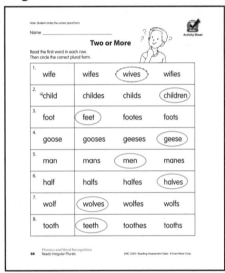

Note: Student circles the correct plural form.

Name _____

### Two or More

Read the first word in each row.
Then circle the correct plural form.

| 1. wife | wifes | (wives) | wifies |
| 2. child | childes | childs | (children) |
| 3. foot | (feet) | footes | foots |
| 4. goose | gooses | geeses | (geese) |
| 5. man | mans | (men) | manes |
| 6. half | halfs | halfes | (halves) |
| 7. wolf | (wolves) | wolfes | wolfs |
| 8. tooth | (teeth) | toothes | tooths |

Phonics and Word Recognition
66 Reads Irregular Plurals                    EMC 3339 • Reading Assessment Tasks • © Evan-Moor Corp.

## Page 72

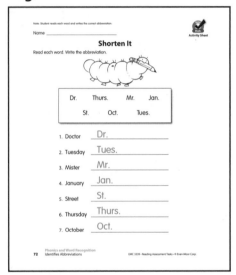

Note: Student reads each word and writes the correct abbreviation.

Name _____

### Shorten It

Read each word. Write the abbreviation.

| Dr. | Thurs. | Mr. | Jan. |
| St. | Oct. | Tues. | |

1. Doctor    Dr.
2. Tuesday   Tues.
3. Mister    Mr.
4. January   Jan.
5. Street    St.
6. Thursday  Thurs.
7. October   Oct.

Phonics and Word Recognition
72 Identifies Abbreviations                   EMC 3339 • Reading Assessment Tasks • © Evan-Moor Corp.

## Page 80

Note: Student says each picture name and writes a blend to complete each word.

Name _____

### Listen for Blends

Name each picture.
Listen to the sounds.
Write the missing letters.

cr    fr    br    gr

1. c r ow
2. f r og
3. f r ame
4. g r apes
5. f r uit
6. g r ay
7. b r own
8. c r ab
9. g r ill

Phonics and Word Recognition
Distinguishes Between Consonant Blends:
80  cr, fr, gr, dr, tr, br                    EMC 3339 • Reading Assessment Tasks • © Evan-Moor Corp.

## Page 88

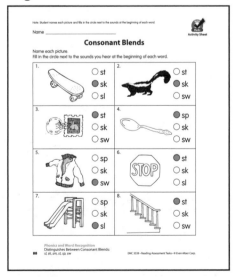

Note: Student names each picture and fills in the circle next to the sounds at the beginning of each word.

Name _____

### Consonant Blends

Name each picture.
Fill in the circle next to the sounds you hear at the beginning of each word.

1. ○ st  ● sk  ○ sl
2. ○ st  ● sk  ○ sw
3. ● st  ○ sk  ○ sw
4. ● sp  ○ sk  ○ sw
5. ○ sp  ○ sk  ● sw
6. ● st  ○ sk  ○ sl
7. ○ sp  ○ sk  ● sl
8. ● st  ○ sk  ○ sw

Phonics and Word Recognition
Distinguishes Between Consonant Blends:
88  sl, sk, sm, st, sp, sw                    EMC 3339 • Reading Assessment Tasks • © Evan-Moor Corp.